The Evolution of Investing at the University of Michigan

1817-2016

Rafael E. Castilla

William P. Hodgeson

Investment Office

University of Michigan

Published in the United States of America by
Michigan Publishing
Manufactured in the United States of America

DOI: http://dx.doi.org/10.3998/mpub.9496949

ISBN 978-1-60785-391-6 (paper)
ISBN 978-1-60785-392-3 (e-book)

An imprint of Michigan Publishing, Maize Books serves the publishing needs of the University of Michigan community by making high-quality scholarship widely available in print and online. It represents a new model for authors seeking to share their work within and beyond the academy, offering streamlined selection, production, and distribution processes. Maize Books is intended as a complement to more formal modes of publication in a wide range of disciplinary areas.
http://www.maizebooks.org

Profits, if any, from the sale of this book will benefit Michigan Publishing and the University of Michigan Library.

To past, current, and future donors through whose collective generosity the University of Michigan has funds to invest. You are all critical to the University's success. Go Blue!

Contents

Acknowledgments

This book would not have been possible without the help and support of many individuals. Special thanks to Felicia David-Visser, Senior Manager of Investments, for her contributions to the section on Working Capital Pools and Other Investments. We also thank each of the following for their numerous contributions:

L. Erik Lundberg, Chief Investment Officer
Michele Everard, Managing Director of Investments
Joan Thowsen, Managing Director of Investments
Michael Haessler, Director of Investments
David Demeter, Manager of Investments
Marcos Esparza, Investment Analyst
Coleen Akemann, Executive Secretary

David J. Brophy, Professor of Finance, Ross School of Business

Jason E. Colman, Director of Michigan Publishing Services
Norman G. Herbert, Investment Officer
Erin Katz, Assistant Secretary of the University
John C. Lofy, Assistant Campaign Director
John Sullivan, Treasurer

Jeffrey Meade, Cambridge Associates

J. Ira Harris, Investment Advisory Committee
Sanford R. Robertson, Investment Advisory Committee

Index of Exhibits

Foreword

This project originated as an internal reference for staff at the Investment Office and others at the University of Michigan, but then grew to be much more. It is not only a thorough history of how investing has developed at the University of Michigan from its inception but also a carefully documented case study on the history and development of institutional investing in general. This fascinating story represents a unique contribution to the history of finance and should have broad appeal to any student of the history of institutional investing in the United States. The book is also the Investment Office's proud contribution to the University of Michigan Bicentennial celebration.

The book creates broad historical context, carefully describing how the University responded to changes in legal regimes, investment theory, and ever-broadening investment opportunities, adjusting its investment management and governance as its portfolio of investments evolved from the early days—consisting mostly of debt securities of companies in Southeast Michigan—to today's multibillion-dollar, globally diversified investment program. This program is managed by a sophisticated, professional staff whom I have had the pleasure to lead for the past decade and a half.

While the story as told is unique to Michigan, Michigan's experience likely is not all that unique in that institutions of higher learning across the country faced the same changing external investment environment and responded in largely similar ways, as we all learn from each other. I am particularly interested in how governance and staffing evolved in response to the growing size and complexity of the University's investment program, with today's dedicated Investment Office being the latest iteration. The process is ongoing. Future changes hopefully will be discussed in an update to this book.

Numerous individuals both within and outside the University contributed to this project. I would like to particularly highlight the contributions of Ira Harris and Sandy Robertson, who have been instrumental in guiding and shaping the University's investment activities from the earliest days of the University's Investment Advisory Committee and deserve much credit for the University's investment success. I'd also like to highlight the contributions of Professor Brophy of the Ross School of Business who, through his tireless efforts over the years, undoubtedly has influenced many a student's decision to pursue a career in investment management or to become a successful entrepreneur.

Erik Lundberg
Chief Investment Officer

CHAPTER ONE

Introduction

This book originated as an internal Investment Office study on the history and evolution of Regental governance over the University of Michigan's investment portfolios. As we delved into the subject matter, it became clear that in order to properly understand the history and evolution of governance, it was necessary to also study and understand the broader history and evolution of investing at the University, which provides the context for the evolution of governance.

Similarly, to more fully understand the broader history of investing at the University, and in turn place *it* in a broader context, it is indispensable to more generally understand some of the history and evolution of institutional investing in the United States (and globally). Thus this book hopes to provide a high-level, yet comprehensive and contextualized, history of the evolution of investing and Regental oversight over investing at the University of Michigan.

Correspondingly, we believe this book may be interesting not just because it describes what transpired at the University of Michigan but also because it can be viewed as a case study illustrating how institutional investing in the Unites States (and globally) has changed and evolved in the past hundred years.

As will be discussed in detail, the role of the Board of Regents in overseeing the University's financial assets has evolved in tandem with investment management law, theory, and practice over the past 80 years: from a strict allocation between direct investments in bonds and a so-called master list of permissible stock investments to the highly diversified multi-asset class and multi-manager strategy employed today—known in the industry as the "endowment model."

Many aspects of the investment of the University's financial assets have evolved, and even changed radically, over time. Summarizing the broader themes, herein we describe the following:

1. How the University's endowment has grown through favorable investment returns, as well as through the establishment of a Development Office and increased gift giving.
2. How the University moved from an "income" to a "total return" approach to investing, which in turn drove changes in the way it allocated assets, managed its distribution policy (separating it from income), and benchmarked its performance.
3. How the University shifted its focus from individual investments and transactions to asset allocation and investment with outside managers.
4. How the Board of Regents concomitantly moved from the approval of individual transactions to the approval of outside investment managers.
5. How the University's endowment transitioned from an almost solely fixed-income oriented portfolio to primarily equity today.
6. How the University diversified into "alternative" asset classes such as distressed debt, private equity, venture capital, real estate, energy and natural resources, absolute return and hedge funds, commodities, currencies, and derivatives.
7. How the Investment Advisory Committee, formed in 1990, supported a transition to alternative assets and to the "endowment model" and otherwise provided invaluable advice to the University.
8. How investing at the University was impacted and influenced by two seminal studies by the Ford Foundation published in 1969, which led to changes in the laws of investing, such as the adoption of the Uniform Management of Institutional Funds Act (UMIFA) and later the Uniform Prudent Management of Institutional Funds Act (UPMIFA); as well as by changes in the theories and practices of investing, such as the advent of Modern Portfolio Theory and the rise and prominence of the "endowment model" of investing.
9. How issues such as proxy voting, South African divestment, and tobacco divestment were addressed.

It should be noted that this book principally focuses on what we term the University's "endowment" portfolio, currently more precisely referred to as the "Long Term Portfolio," or the LTP. There are several reasons for this. Most important, a majority of the University's pure investment assets (i.e., assets not including capital assets that it utilizes in its operations such as buildings, equipment, and collections) have always been in the endowment portfolio. Second, the endowment portfolio constitutes the University's "permanent" corpus of investment, so this is where the more innovative long-term investment programs have been introduced. Correspondingly, the endowment portfolio has received the most high-level coverage, whether in the meeting minutes of the Board of Regents, in the annual Reports of Investments, or among the University community and even external community and press at large.

Nonetheless, we include a section toward the end that also describes the University's working capital portfolios, as well as some other University and University-affiliated investment vehicles.

While reading this book, one may want to reference the following chart that traces the size of the endowment from 1930 through 2016, in 2016 U.S. dollars according to a CPI index adjustment:

Real Value of the Endowment 1930–2016

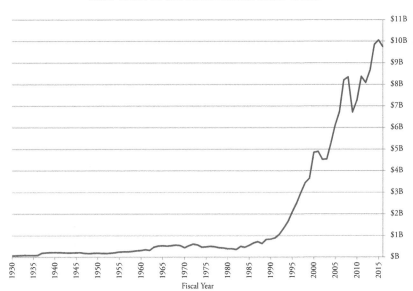

1930-1944: Book value of Endowment
1945-1987: Market value of Endowment and Other Invested Assets
1988-2016: Market value of Endowment Funds

CHAPTER TWO

From 1817 Through the 1970s
The Early Years

T he University of Michigan obviously had assets and funds, and thus some form of investments, since the establishment of its predecessor, the "Catholepistemiad of Michigania," in 1817. However, it is not until 1928 that we find a record of what is now called the "Report of Investments" (ROI), and that is where we will begin a more detailed treatment of the evolution of investing. But nonetheless, a few interesting words can first be said about the University's financial governance and history prior to 1928.

From 1817 until 1837, the "Catholepistemiad of Michigania" had a fragmented history. In fact, it seemed to essentially cease operating around 1827. During this period of limited operations, the institution appears to have been funded primarily via land grants (including a foundational land grant from the federal government under the Treaty of Fort Meigs) and donations (including for example an early $250 gift from the Freemason Zion Lodge No. 1 of Detroit). Land was periodically sold off to fund the institution.

In 1825, the Erie Canal was completed, opening up trade between the East coast and the Great Lakes regions. At the beginning of 1837, the State of Michigan was admitted to the Union. This same year the University of Michigan was established, or reestablished, pursuant to the Organic Act of March 18, 1837, in Ann Arbor, where the first meeting of the Board of Regents was held on June 5, 1837.

The first real "endowment" of the University of Michigan may have been a significant land grant gifted to it, again by the federal government of the United

States on May 20, 1826 in "an Act concerning a seminary of learning in the territory of Michigan." It was not long after the University was truly launched in 1837 that the first questions regarding the proper use of this "endowment" arose. In a January 1839 meeting of the Board of Regents, a report was presented regarding "the legality of appropriations made out of the fund derived from the sale of University Lands for the support of University Branches." "University Branches" are a fascinating, and critical, early initiative of the University of Michigan whereby the University established and controlled what were essentially preparatory high schools throughout Michigan, to act as feeders for the new University. Otherwise, at this time, as one might imagine, secondary education, to the extent it existed in Michigan, was not designed to prepare students for higher education. Thus the University of Michigan played a critical role not only in the development of higher education but also in the development of secondary education in the State of Michigan.[1]

In 1850, the State of Michigan adopted a new state constitution. Article 13, entitled "Education," made two important changes. The Board of Regents would now be separately and democratically elected, and the office of President of the University was created. Although governance had already gone through various iterations, immediately prior to 1850 the Board of Regents had been appointed by the Governor and had included the Governor himself and other members of state government, including Justices of the Michigan Supreme Court. Thus management of the University, including financial management, was entangled with other branches of state government—a reality that was bemoaned in the minutes of more than one Regental meeting. Now the University was constituted

---

1   Echoing the later famous statement of President James Angell regarding the University providing "an uncommon education for the common man" (and today, also woman), the 1839 report explained:

> The evil had long been perceived by the people of the United States that College education, maintained by the Public Funds of the different States, was principally confined to the children of the wealthy who could afford to send and maintain their sons at such Institutions. But all alike had not the same advantage, and many a stupid heir of Fortune received the parchment title of an A.B. or an A.S.S., when impoverished genius and talent had to struggle on without this Public facility. Congress, in this Act, determined differently in the appropriation of this portion of the Public domain for the use of a University designed for the education of the People of the Peninsula of Michigan.

as a kind of independent fourth branch of government—and its financial management fell squarely and exclusively within the purview of the Board of Regents. This structure, as we will see, would years later in 1988 be litigated in connection with the divest South Africa movement.

In 1851, the Michigan legislature passed a new statute reestablishing the University of Michigan—this is the Act that governs the University of Michigan to this day. Three of the 23 sections of the Act contain the term "university fund" in the title and, in addition, various other sections refer to the use of interest on the university fund. The "university fund" may thus be regarded as the predecessor to what is now referred to as the "University Endowment Fund," or UEF, the main endowment fund of the University, which is discussed in greater detail below. In 1852, Henry Philip Tappan was appointed the first University President.

In 1867, the first mill tax was established, and the University of Michigan has received some form of appropriation or other financial support from the State of Michigan ever since.

From early on, the University of Michigan also had the good fortune of attracting more private gifts than perhaps the typical public institution of the time:

> *With the advent of the state universities of a later era the fact that support was given them at first through government land grants and then later by the states, or in some cases by municipalities, tended to limit the development of private gifts. At the present time only a few of the state universities have received any great degree of support from private benefactors. Almost from the beginning, the University of Michigan, with its long record of gifts from private citizens and particularly from alumni, has been an exception. There are a few state universities which have received large gifts, notably California, but these have come mostly from private donors rather than from the alumni, and although exact figures, particularly on alumni gifts, are not easily available, it may be said that Michigan has received far more from her alumni than any other state institution.*[2]

Toward the end of the 19th century and the beginning of the 20th, "the era of spectacular contributions to the University was inaugurated." The first true

---

2   W. Shaw, *The University of Michigan, An Encyclopedic Survey* (Ann Arbor, MI: University of Michigan), pp. 185–86.

endowments were established, a long list of loan and scholarship funds was created, the Michigan Union and the Michigan League were constructed, and other gifts were used to build additional facilities, collections, and libraries.[3]

By 1928—the year in which the "Consolidated Endowment Fund" was first established and the first year for which we have a ROI—the financial assets accumulated such that the University had some $4 million in financial assets. The 1928 ROI was more a list of investments than a report, and it was called "Investments of all Deposit Accounts & Trust Funds." There were four groupings of fund types:

    i.   Deposit Accounts in Custody of the Treasurer
    ii.   Endowment Funds
    iii.   Expendable Funds
    iv.   Student Loan Funds

Investments had the following classifications:

    i.   Cash
    ii.   Certificate of Deposit
    iii.   Bonds
    iv.   Contracts
    v.   Mortgages
    vi.   Real Estate
    vii.   Stocks
    viii.   Student Loans
    ix.   Tuition Notes

Of the $4,093,293.52 listed of total funds, 10.7% was invested in Cash or Certificates of Deposit, and 80.5% was invested in Bonds, Mortgages, and Real Estate. Stocks were 3.1% and Student Loans 2.9%. Other categories (mainly Contracts; see below) were 2.8%. The stocks were likely not acquired by purchase by the University but presumably acquired as gifts. Endowment Funds were about $2.7 million of the total.

Every investment of every internal unit was separately listed. "Mortgages" were single mortgages, not pools, many of them loans to the University's own

---

3   Shaw, *The University of Michigan, An Encyclopedic Survey*, p. 188.

faculty and staff under a special program that no longer exists. A number of "bonds" were issued by banks and, interestingly, also appear to be backed by specific mortgages, which are listed. Other bonds were secured corporate loans. Generally speaking, investments were local to Southern Michigan, although there were many exceptions. The Lawyers' Club held bonds issued by the Kingdom of Norway and the Martha Cook Dormitory held bonds issued by the United Kingdom of Great Britain and Ireland. Edison-affiliated companies appear in numerous places. There are bonds issued by the City of Toronto, the State of Queensland (Australia), Florida Power & Light Company, and various other utilities and railroad investments, for example. So, to an extent, the University was already investing nationally and even internationally.

The "Levi Barbour Oriental Girls Scholarship" held many of the "Contracts," which also appear to be mortgages, but on undeveloped lots. And although the name may now sound anachronistic, it was a very progressive idea at the time:

> *President Ruthven has characterized the University of Michigan's Barbour Scholarships for Oriental Women as a unique possession. In the long list of scholarships and fellowships for foreign students in the United States nothing comparable in number and widespread influence can be found. Some 212 women have been provided University training, qualifying them to return for lives of service in their homelands. They come from a dozen countries, spanning Asia to Istanbul. Their service literally encircles the globe: they are in Hawaii, Japan, Korea, China, the Philippines, Thailand, Malaya, India, Syria, and Turkey, with a few in Europe and a number in the United States.*[4]

Of the small allocation to equities, there were stock investments in, for example, various railroads, Detroit Chemical Works, White Star Line, and Grayling Lumber Company.

The end of the report contained listings "showing all bonds acquired during the year" and listings "showing all bonds sold, redeemed or otherwise disposed of during the year."

Before continuing the history, we pause for an important observation. From inception through November 1986 (see below), there was a crucial practice that drove many aspects of endowment management, including spending policy. This was the practice of distributing *income as actually generated by the*

---

4 Shaw, *The University of Michigan, An Encyclopedic Survey*, p. 185.

portfolio, whether in the form of interest or dividends, to endowment beneficiaries. Of course, this practice was not undertaken arbitrarily but reflected
the general practice of the times which, in turn, reflected the historical law of
trusts. Under the old law of trusts, when a principal-protected (i.e., permanent)
gift to an institution was made, the language was both written and interpreted
so as to constrain the beneficiary in the institution to only receive and spend
the *income* generated by the underlying assets in any given year. Thus even
if the underlying assets had *appreciated* in market value, the *principal* could *not*,
whether in part or in whole, be liquidated and spent. This policy could constrain an institution's spending even if its investments had done very well. On
the other hand, these gifts could also constrain an institution's spending policy
by in effect *requiring* income to be distributed to the gift beneficiaries—even if
the principal had *depreciated* in value or if the income was more than required.
These beneficiaries were of course always free to reinvest "excess" income back
into the endowment or some other portfolio but, life being what it is, might
have chosen to spend it instead.

The income approach was eventually replaced in law, gift instruments, and
practice, both at the University of Michigan (as described below) and at other
institutions, by the *total return approach*, whereby the focus would be on a portfolio's total return (income *taken together with* appreciation/depreciation), which
would then be divorced from short-term spending. Spending policy could then
be set separately and reviewed periodically. Of course, over the long run, the two
concepts of total return and spending must remain connected as one can only
ultimately spend what one has made.

Summarizing important differences between the two approaches:

1. As mentioned, under the income approach, spending policy (often
    called "distribution policy," which sounds less profligate) was linked
    lockstep to investment policy, with numerous consequences. Distri-
    butions might be higher or lower than optimal or desired and could
    fluctuate from year to year in unexpected fashion. In contrast, under
    the total return approach, spending policy can be divorced from
    income considerations, be made stable and predictable, and the port-
    folio can be managed for the long term on a total return basis, with the
    focus on targeting the appropriate overall risk/return profile to meet
    the spending policy in the long term.

2. Related to the prior point, the total return approach allows spending policy to target the long-term preservation of the *real* value of the endowment. Under this approach, which is common at many institutions, spending policy is conservatively targeted to be less than, or equal to, the expected long-term return on the endowment minus expected inflation.

3. Under the income approach, investments might be made on the basis of how much stable income they produced as opposed to what total return they might generate, or what risk/return characteristics they brought to the portfolio. There is thus a natural bias toward fixed income and more conservative investments under the income approach, and a bias toward equity and more aggressive investments under the total return approach.

4. The income approach involved less emphasis on market value and total return and, therefore, tended to focus on the traditional accounting concepts of book value and income return. Thus we see that even through 1992, the University's investment reports contained book value information for its investments. And it was not until 1977 that the University started publishing total market value returns regularly for its main endowment fund. In current investment management practice, there is an almost singular focus on total return.

5. The total return approach invites a greater degree and precision of benchmarking and relative comparison of performance, both of investment managers and across institutions. Without digressing too much, we note that widespread adoption of benchmarking has contributed to deep changes in the investment management industry, including making it more competitive and professionalized and allowing for complex structuring of performance-linked incentive compensation for investment managers.[5]

6. Finally, of less direct importance but interesting nonetheless, the widespread adoption of total return investing has been found to have contributed to changing dividend policy at public corporations. When equity securities were bought primarily for income there was greater pressure on, and incentive for, the issuers of these securities to distribute free cash

---

5   The S&P 500 index took its current form in 1957.

flow to their equity investors. The adoption of total return investing has changed investing, corporate policy, and management in other ways, a comprehensive analysis of which is beyond the scope of this book.

An internal Investment Office report from May 1952 summarized the old income approach nicely:

> *Endowment funds by their nature are expected to endure for a long period of years. It is generally expected that the principal of such funds must be maintained intact and only the income expended for the particular purpose for which the endowment is created. Thus, it is possible to take a long range approach to the investments of such funds. There is no problem of meeting any future obligations out of the principal, and the fluctuations of security prices are not of great importance except, of course, as they provide opportunities to buy and sell or switch from one type of investment to another. . . . It is apparent, however, that to accomplish the purposes for which these funds have been established, income is of prime importance, not only from the standpoint of amount but also of stability.*

Continuing now with the history, in November 1931, the Board of Regents adopted two new resolutions authorizing any two of the four listed University officers, *with the prior approval of the Finance Committee or of the Board of Regents as a whole*, to sell investment securities on behalf of the University. The listed University officers were (i) the President, (ii) the Vice President and Secretary, (iii) the Controller and Assistant Secretary, and (iv) the Investment Officer. We say "new" resolutions because they do not appear to replace any language that might have been in place previously. These resolutions were incorporated into the University's Bylaws in 1940 and, despite numerous revisions and movements, much of the same—now highly antiquated—language remains in place today. A couple of months before the passage of these resolutions, in September 1931, the University had created the position of Investment Officer and named its first one, Julius E. Schmidt.

Note that the focus of these resolutions was on *selling* investments, not buying them. This might be because at this point in time the University was either keeping gifts of securities long-term for their income stream (which included, in the case of debt securities, eventual redemption) or occasionally liquidating them for cash. Making *new* investments with cash may have been less of a focus—although it certainly also happened.

Finally, note that the role of the Board of Regents (or its Finance Committee) was in relation to the investments themselves—not in relation to *investment managers,* as is the case now. In fact, it appears that at this time the University did not have any outside investment managers whatsoever—not surprising for this point in the history of investing.

Buying and selling efficiently and in volume requires developed and liquid capital markets. In 1933, the Securities Act (regulating securities registration) became law in the United States and, in 1934, Congress passed the Securities Exchange Act (regulating securities trading). In 1939, the Trust Indenture Act (regulating bond indentures) was passed and, in 1940, the Investment Advisers Act (regulating investment managers) and the Investment Company Act (regulating mutual funds) were passed. This suite of legislation formed the basis for the explosive development and growth of the securities markets in the United States and contributed to giving the U.S. economy—and investing—a modern structure. Over time, many other countries would emulate the U.S. capital markets model.

In April 1936, the Board of Regents approved the *purchase* of up to a 10% allocation to common stocks—supporting our prior inference that *purchasing* securities (particularly purchasing stocks) was historically a less common transaction than *selling* securities. Thus began a relentless, multidecade process of converting the University's endowment portfolios from almost all fixed income to mostly equity today.

The common stocks were to be chosen from a list of "approved common stocks of high grade, regarded as proper investments for trust funds under the decisions of the Michigan Supreme Court. . . . All such investments are to be with the approval of the Finance Committee." This reference to a so-called "legal list" of "high grade" common stocks reflects the then prevailing trust law in Michigan and throughout much of the country that deemed certain investments as improperly speculative and thus impermissible for trusts *per se*—that is, as a matter of law. Thus no common stock could be purchased unless it was included in the legal list and with the actual transaction also being approved by the Finance Committee of the Board of Regents.

As a note, the University's "Endowment Funds" had a book value at this time (1936) of $4.2 million, equivalent to about $73.9 million in 2016 U.S. dollars according to a CPI index adjustment.

Interestingly, just one year later in 1937, the State of Michigan became one of the earlier adopters via statute of the so-called Prudent Man Rule (now known as the Prudent Investor Rule), whereby legal lists for trustees were abolished and the "prudent man" standard (i.e., good fiduciary judgment) was required to be applied instead.[6] Nonetheless, the University *practice* of using a "Master List" (as it was called) for common stocks did not die so easily—it was probably around this time that the Master List became an *internal* construct, rather than one mandated by state law and regulation. In fact, as we shall see, the Master List lived on for almost another half century, until November 1986.

By July 1940, the above-described November 1931 resolutions had been recast and incorporated into the University's Bylaws as Sections 3.16 and 3.17. In July 1945, the Bylaws were again recast and renumbered, with technical changes.

It is interesting to note that during the years of World War II, 1939 to 1945, the Reports of Investments do not appear to contain a single reference to this great war. What a different time! Currently, even minor political crises (certainly relative to World War II) tend to give rise to profuse economic and market analyses. One can come up with various reasons why this might be the case: the ways in which the media has changed, the ways in which investing has changed, and the ways in which investments are viewed has changed. A full analysis would take us beyond the scope of this book.

In the minutes of the February 1952 meeting of the Board of Regents, there is a short but important reference. The Board

authorized the employment of the trust department of the National Bank of Detroit (NBD) for advice and consultation in regard to the investment of a portion of the University's endowment funds. The services will also include custody of the securities of these funds.

This defining event marks the University's initial entry into the era of modern investment management. It occurs 15 years after the adoption by the State

---

6   The Prudent Man Rule found its first formulation in the famous case of *Harvard College v. Amory*, 26 Mass. 446 (1830)—which, interestingly, involved an endowment. It took many years, well into the twentieth century, however, for this rule to replace the legal list statutes in all of the states of the United States. The case was decided in Boston, Massachusetts, which was at the time, and remains to this day, a U.S. center for fiduciary asset management. In analyzing the impossibility of preserving principal under all possible future scenarios, it contains perhaps the most famous line in U.S. investment management law: "Do what you will, the capital is at hazard."

of Michigan of the Prudent Man Rule (now more commonly known as the Prudent Investor Rule), not quite 20 years after the passage of the Securities Act of 1933 and of the Securities Exchange Act of 1934, and in the very same year that Harry Markowitz published his seminal paper on Modern Portfolio Theory in the *Journal of Finance*. Also, this is the first reference we discovered to an outside investment adviser being formally engaged on an ongoing basis by the University.

One might infer that prior to 1952 it was the University's Investment Office that was, with the approval of the Finance Committee, directly involved in selecting most of the University's securities, perhaps with occasional outside consultations—with a reiteration that in any case there would have been a limited amount of *purchases* of equities. After 1952, with the appointment of NBD, there began a trend whereby the Investment Office became more focused on selecting advisors and vehicles, and setting strategy and asset allocation, rather than on selecting the securities themselves.

A few months later, in May 1952, and perhaps related to the new relationship with NBD, the Bylaws relating to investing (now renumbered) were again amended, *removing the requirement for Finance Committee approval of all investment transactions*. However, all transactions were still to be reported to the Board of Regents at the following meeting. Nonetheless, as we shall see, despite this revision of the Bylaws, it seems that the Board of Regents continued ratifying investment transactions after the fact, as well as changes to the Master List. But perhaps the processes were simplified at this time.

A May 1952 report disclosed that the University now held 13% of its endowment funds in common stock. It recommended an "Intermediate Objective" for the next 2 to 3 years that included a target of 35% to common stocks. A "Possible Long-Term Objective" targeted a 45% allocation to common stocks. Though not termed as such, these objectives could be thought of as a predecessor to the current concept of Model Portfolio. In this connection, it is interesting to note that the University reviewed "a study of twelve large endowment funds of educational institutions [that] was presented at a meeting of the Central Association of College and University Business Officers"—an early example of benchmarking to other institutions. At this point in time, the University of Michigan was significantly "behind" in its equity allocation as compared to other higher education institutions, which averaged 43% as of the end of 1951—in general, private institutions were earlier investors in equity securities than public ones.

In June 1953, the Board of Regents unitized the Consolidated Endowment Fund (CEF). Like with a mutual fund, University departments and other units with an interest in the CEF would now hold internal "shares" that could be acquired or redeemed. This change would serve to ease and make uniform the accounting, administration, and investment of endowment monies. To this day, all major University portfolios are unitized.

In 1958, the U.S. Congress created the Small Business Investment Company (SBIC) program to facilitate the flow of long-term capital to America's small businesses. The creation of the SBIC program was a seminal step in the development of the professional venture capital industry. As we shall see, decades later the University would participate as an investor in this new, as well as other new, asset classes, as the University diversified into alternative investments.

In February 1968, all of the University's Bylaws were reorganized, but with no significant changes to the investment Bylaws. In July 1968, the Bylaws were tweaked to relax the resolution specifying which two officers could execute purchases and sales. Also in 1968, the Report of Investments finally stopped listing individual endowments. As a result, this 1968 report went down to 7 pages in length from 102 pages the prior year, though the length would again increase in the future.

In December 1969, the Board of Regents approved the creation of a new, separate investment pool within the endowment. The June 30, 1970 Report of Investments explained that this new pool, termed "Funds Functioning as Endowments" or, alternatively, "Total Return Fund," would be "operated on the 'Total Return' concept."[7] This development represents (i) the first point in time the University would explicitly start managing a portion of its investment funds on a total return, as opposed to income, basis and (ii) the birth of the concept of identifying funds that are *not* "true" endowment funds, but which will nonetheless be managed for the very long term in parallel with permanent endowment funds. This same concept would be extended in 1994 to an investment by the University's operating funds, at that time called the "University Investment Pool," or UIP. These investments of nonendowment funds into the endowment portfolio are now commonly termed "quasi-endowments."

In 1970, still 6 years before the passage of the Uniform Management of Institutional Funds Act (UMIFA, see below), the University was still operating under the legal advice that it was not permissible to invest "true" endowment funds on

---

7   The amount of this new Total Return Fund was initially approximately $11 million, or about 27% of the existing endowment funds.

a total return basis, so, wanting to adopt the total return approach to the extent permissible, it segregated funds that were not "true" endowments in order to do so. As we shall see, by the early 1980s, *all* of the University's funds would be invested on a total return basis.

Now we turn to two areas of investment policy that the Board of Regents has retained to this day: proxy voting and divestment policy. Both of these areas lay dormant as a subject of active engagement until the turbulent era of the 1970s.

In April 1971, the Board of Regents addressed proxy voting in connection with "Campaign GM" initiated by Ralph Nader and driven by automotive safety concerns. This campaign has been called by some the inauguration of the consumer movement for corporate responsibility. One of the campaign's initiatives involved proxy voting resolutions. At this time the Board of Regents reviewed, and reaffirmed, the University's policy on voting proxies.

This policy, although refined over time, has not changed substantially and states, in summary, that the University votes on specific items with management, unless voting with management would be against the financial interest of the University, in which case the University would vote against management or consider selling its position. There has to date never been a general consideration of social or political issues in connection with proxy voting unless the Board of Regents has given specific direction. Thus the University did not support the Campaign GM resolutions, stating:

> *We understand the deep concerns expressed on this matter. It is apparent that the number of corporate or government practices which some members of the society find offensive are almost unlimited. On the other hand, the complaints which are made about corporate and government practices are matters of public policy. They can be, and are, subject to regulations and change by legislation at the federal, state, or local level. Under our system, the law changes with the times and is equally applicable to all parties. This has been evident during the past years with respect to problems of pollution, minority employment, safety issues, etc.*

In 1978, the Board of Regents considered its first divestment proposal in connection with Apartheid in South Africa.[8] An extended examination of the complex

---

8   The anti-Apartheid divestment campaign on university campuses began on the West Coast and in the Midwest in 1977, at Stanford and Michigan State Universities. In 1978, Michigan State University voted in favor of total divestiture.

history of this issue, which played out over years and appeared to be contentious, is beyond the scope of this book; however, we do summarize the deliberations because important policy, still in place to this day, was set at this time.

In March 1978, the Board of Regents stopped short of directing full divestiture from South Africa but adopted numerous related resolutions, as well as affirmed the so-called Sullivan Principles, as recommended in a report on "Investment Policies and Social Responsibility" presented by the Senate Assembly Advisory Committee on Financial Affairs. Importantly, these resolutions in effect set a general policy and process for consideration by the Board of Regents of social investing issues, to be applied going forward:

> *If the Regents shall determine that a particular issue involves serious moral or ethical questions which are of concern to many members of the University community, an advisory committee consisting of members of the University Senate, students, administration and alumni will be appointed to gather information and formulate recommendations for the Regents' consideration.*

Six months later, in September 1978, the Board of Regents considered a motion to study whether the University should form a *standing* (permanent) "investment advisory committee on social responsibility and investment policy"—in contrast to the ad hoc approach they had approved 6 months earlier. The motion did not pass. One Regent felt that

> *the thrust of the motion in its general sense is absolutely contrary to what the Senate committee recommended and contrary to regental action last spring. If other issues should arise which affect fundamental human rights and liberties and are broad concerns to the campus community, then an ad hoc committee would again be appointed to study the issues and appropriate action would be taken.*

In 1982, the Michigan legislature passed Act 512, which in effect *required* the University of Michigan to divest from companies operating in South Africa. At the April 1983 meeting, the Board of Regents in fact finally voted to divest—except, that is, from corporations headquartered in Michigan. Although one Regent stated that "the reason why the majority of the Board determined to divest from South Africa was because they truly felt it was the best thing to do.

Not because the legislature told the University to do it," it is clear that the legislative action had a critical impact in terms of the balance of power among Regents with respect to this issue. One Regent lamented "the tragic result of the . . . viral political infection from Lansing . . . politicizing . . . this University for international political goals." Yet at the same time that the Board of Regents voted to divest, it *also* voted to mount a constitutional challenge to the legislative action, on the basis that the State of Michigan did not have constitutional authority to dictate investment policy to the University of Michigan. Five years later, the University won; see *Regents of the University of Michigan v. State of Michigan*, 166 Mich. App. 314 (1988).

One Regent noted a perennial argument against divestment proposals:

A compelling argument, and one which on its merits alone demands that the University not divest, is the legal concept known as the "prudent man rule." That rule of law calls upon those who have a fiduciary responsibility for public or private monies, as the Regents do, [to] knowingly take no actions which may cause damage to the assets in their charge. The Regents have a fiduciary responsibility and are by law required to protect and obtain the best possible return on University investments.

According to the notes from the November 1985 meeting, as a result of the divestment directive, "the University was excluded [from] two-thirds of the Standard and Poor's 500 stock index because of the limitations of the South African divestment policy." If this is accurate, the impact on the University's portfolio and investment choices must have been substantial. In fact, the South African divestment restrictions were in place until November 1993, a full 10 years of operating a South Africa–constrained portfolio! These restrictions had a notable impact on the University's investment returns during this period. As the meeting notes of the Investment Advisory Committee[9] from February 1991 noted:

[Regent] Baker pointed out that the policy prohibiting equity investment in companies with operations in South Africa has cost the portfolio money. . . . the staff has provided information on that cost in percentage terms . . . [Regent] Smith

---

9   See Chapter 7 for a detailed discussion of the Investment Advisory Committee, formed in 1990.

asked why the University had such a policy, and Mr. Herbert replied that it was a
Regental decision and not one recommended by the investment staff.

There is logic to the fact that an elected Board of Regents has retained
authority over these two areas of potentially high public visibility—proxy
voting and divestment. As can be seen from the described examples, they are
two areas of investment policy with potential implications that extend beyond
purely financial considerations of the portfolios (such as risk/return profile,
asset allocation, and diversification), so it is logical that the Board of Regents,
as the ultimate arbiter of University policies, retains its power of review in
these areas.

In 1976, the State of Michigan became an early adopter of UMIFA, first
promulgated in 1972 by the National Conference of Commissioners on Uniform
State Laws.[10] The driving idea was to codify in a uniform way for the nonprofit
sector the Prudent Investor Rule, which had already replaced the legal lists in
many U.S. states. This rule had also been in effect codified under the Employee
Retirement Income Security Act of 1974 (ERISA), the federal law regulating
private pensions. Whereas previously nonprofit institutions in the management
of their funds had generally been subject to the broader case law of trusts, now
they would be governed by a statute customized to their particular circumstances
and issues.

Among other things, UMIFA provisions made it clear that a "governing
board" (in the case of the University of Michigan, the Board of Regents) could
invest in pooled vehicles where "investment determinations are made by persons
other than the governing board" and could "delegate to its committees, officers,
or employees of the institution or the fund, or agents, including investment

---

10 The publication of two influential reports concerning college endowments by the Ford
    Foundation acted as a catalyst for this Uniform Act: W. Cary & C. Bright, *The Law and the
    Lore of Endowment Funds* (Ford Foundation, 1969); and Advisory Committee on Endow-
    ment Management to the Ford Foundation, *Managing Educational Endowments* (Ford
    Foundation, 1969). In fact, these reports were specifically cited in the December 1969
    Request for Action approving the creation of a Funds Functioning as Endowment pool to
    be managed on a total return basis. Another publication was quite influential with respect
    to spending policy: R. Ennis & P. Williamson, *Spending Policy for Educational Endow-
    ments: A Research and Publication Project of The Common Fund* (New York: The Common
    Fund, 1976).

counsel, the authority to act in place of the board in investment and reinvestment of institutional funds."

Again moving away from historical trust law, UMIFA also restated a governing board's standard of care as being one of "ordinary business care and prudence under the facts and circumstances prevailing at the time of the action or decision." The accompanying comment to the model code explained that this "standard is generally comparable to that of a director of a business corporation rather than that of a private trustee." Historical trust law generally contained standards of care that were more onerous and less flexible for trustees.

These provisions in UMIFA explicitly allowed for the delegation of investment decision making and the ability to invest in pooled vehicles and corporatized the standard of care—both natural consequences of the reality of investment management becoming more complex, international, and professionalized, with more options, securities, alternative investments, specializations, asset classes, countries, and currencies from which to choose.

Finally, a provision of UMIFA authorized the governing board to

appropriate for expenditure for the uses and purposes for which an endowment is established so much of the net appreciation, realized and unrealized, in the fair value of the assets of an endowment fund over the historic dollar value of the fund as is prudent.

This was another key, and together with additional provisions in UMIFA permitting the broad interpretation of the language in gift instruments, it opened the door for the adoption by institutions of the total return approach to investment and distribution policy. Although, as previously described, the University of Michigan had already taken steps in that direction, it would go fully total return in November 1986.

Thus Michigan's passage of UMIFA set the stage for and enabled the big changes that were to come in the following two decades in the management and oversight of the University's investments.

As a first step, in November 1978, the Board of Regents appointed the Financial Control Systems Division of Michigan Corporation, later known as the Wellesley Group, "to evaluate the investment programs of the University's endowment funds." This is the first reference we found to the engagement of what we now term "investment consultants."

CHAPTER THREE

The 1980s
The Great Transition

In the 1980s, the University took its first steps toward modern institutional asset management with broader diversification into various asset classes, including alternative assets, the engagement of multiple managers, regular application of benchmarking to indices, and some key changes in the Board of Regents' oversight of investments, such as the move to approving managers rather than transactions.

In February 1981, the Board of Regents first authorized a securities lending program in order to generate incremental income. The minutes of this meeting reflect some conflation of the concepts of total return investing versus asset allocation percentages. It seemed to be believed that adopting a total return approach required having no asset allocation percentages for public securities,[1] so it seems that for a few years at least, percentage limitations were removed. In any case, total return investing would be more explicitly adopted a few years later, as discussed below.

In March 1982, the Board of Regents authorized (i) a 5% allocation to the Common Fund for Equities, (ii) numerous additions to the "Master List of Common Stocks" (the names of many are not even recognizable today), (iii) a "buy-write" (options writing) program, and (iv) a 5% allocation to

---

1   In fact, strictly applying Modern Portfolio Theory, this would be correct not just for public securities but for the entire portfolio. Perhaps this is the origin of the idea.

real estate "through partnerships or commingled funds," including specifically authorizing an investment in the Endowment and Foundation Realty
Partnership—JMB I.

In January 1983, the Board of Regents was presented the basics of venture
capital investing. It is instructive to review this extended excerpt, which places
the thinking at that time in perspective to today's:

> *Vice-President Brinkerhoff commented upon the request to participate in venture
> capital investment opportunities. He said this was the result of several years of
> exploration of investment opportunities in this field. Doan Associates is one of the
> oldest venture capital organizations in the state of Michigan and its activities are
> focused largely within the State.*
>
> *Norman Herbert, University investment officer, briefly summarized the con-
> cept of venture capital investment. He said it is a term defined as a high risk, high
> potential return investment in nonmarketable securities usually in small compa-
> nies whose future performances are considered to be favorable. He explained the
> meaning of a limited partnership and noted that the rewards from this type of
> investment would not be realized for several years. The recommendation asks for a
> commitment of up to 5% of the University's endowment funds. The primary con-
> centration would be in companies in the state of Michigan in the fields of the life
> sciences, industrial automation, and communication. Investment opportunities,
> however, would not be restricted to these fields nor entirely to the state of Michigan.*
>
> *During the discussion that followed, Regents Baker, Nederlander, and Varner
> expressed their concerns with respect to the limited partnership concept and of
> committing University resources to this type of a venture. They asked for informa-
> tion on specific results other institutions have had, how many investors would be
> involved, and for a prospectus.*
>
> *Regent Roach indicated that, in his view, this particular group of sponsors has an
> excellent record. It should be understood, however, that the University cannot change
> its mind in a few months and expect a return of the invested money. He said that
> not all of the investments would be successful, but it is highly likely that the few that
> are successful would be profitable. Strictly from an investment standpoint, he felt the
> Regents should support the recommendation.*
>
> *President Shapiro remarked that further information would be provided to the
> Regents in response to their concerns before taking action on this issue.*

The next month, in February 1983, the Board of Regents did in fact approve the proposed diversification of endowment assets into venture capital through an investment into the Michigan Investment Fund Limited Partnership. The discussion noted, among other things, "the need for the University to begin taking some risks." However, the prior month's request was changed, as it appears that the Board of Regents was not yet comfortable with approving a fixed allocation; instead, it was determined that "each recommendation for participation in a venture capital limited partnership would be submitted to the Regents for approval." This methodology foreshadowed the current practice today, whereby the Board of Regents actively approves not overall allocations or the Model Portfolio but rather new managers.

The February 1984 meeting was an important one. To fully understand the record of this proceeding, it is helpful to keep in mind that the term "investment adviser" appears to be utilized with a meaning that corresponds more with what is generally currently referred to as "investment consultant"—that is, a third party that does not actively manage money for the University but rather consults with respect to such issues as the selection and supervision of investments and managers, asset allocation, benchmarks, performance and performance attribution, and so on. In February 1984, the National Bank of Detroit (NBD) was appointed as "investment manager" for "80% to 90%" of the University's investment portfolio, indicating it would take a more direct role in the selection of securities. Prior to this, since NBD's appointment in 1952, NBD had been regarded as an "investment adviser" (i.e., investment consultant) only.[2]

Nonetheless, the change, though important for the direction it indicated, was mainly operational, as it is clear that NBD had already been very active in maintaining the Master List and helping select investments for the University. However, until this point, it seems Board of Regents approval, or at least ratification, had always been required both to put stocks on the Master List and to purchase and sell them—even though the requirement had actually been *removed* from the Bylaws in 1952, as discussed above. But by 1984, it seems this laborious process was finally recognized as having become too impractical for the realities of modern investing. Going forward, the Board of Regents would only need to *ratify*

---

2   The terminology is particularly confusing because the legal term for "investment manager" is in fact "investment adviser"—for example, the "Investment Advisers Act of 1940."

changes to the Master List and stock transactions after the fact; preapproval was definitively eliminated—but in any case, the Master List would soon be gone. The University's Investment Officer assured that "it would be very doubtful that an acquisition would be made by NBD that had not been reviewed in advance by the investment office"—demonstrating that the Investment Office was still very involved in security selection at this time.

Thus the Master List, though not discarded quite yet, was showing strains. There are references to investing outside the Master List in "opportunity fund type stocks"—it appears the Opportunity Fund was managed by NBD. Stocks selected for this fund—which we might imagine were lower-rated, more growth-oriented securities—appear to also have been permissible for selection for the University's portfolios since the March 1982 meeting, subject to certain percentage limits. In February 1984, this limit was increased from 5% of the *total common stocks market value* to a maximum of 15% of the same.

At the same time that NBD was given greater investment authority over a large portion of the University's portfolios, it was made clear that this arrangement was only "the first step in bringing about a broader diversification of management responsibility and to possibly bring in other investment managers where appropriate." The Vice President and Chief Financial Officer "would be studying the appropriateness of a variety of investment managers and would periodically report to the University his recommendations."

Finally, at the February 1984 meeting, in a tweak to the proxy voting policy that had been adopted in February 1979, and following the years dealing with the South African issue, it was determined that the University would "abstain on shareholder proposals regarding social responsibility issues" pending further review of the broader issue. Abstention remains the policy on social and political issues to this day.[3]

If one were to point to a single meeting of the Board of Regents that marked the transition between the old and new regimes of investment management, November 1985 would be it. Following on the meetings of the year before, and

---

3   A Request for Action was approved in March 1988 that affirmed the proxy voting policy, as well as provided detailed directives. The impetus for this item was the wave of anti-takeover (and arguably anti-shareholder) measures that were sweeping corporate America, as discussed at the November 1986 Regents meeting (see below). In December 1994, a Request for Action provided for the delegation of proxy voting to managers—until that point in time all proxy voting had been handled by the Investment Office.

after much discussion and with some dissension, the Board of Regents voted, among other things,

> *that the management of the endowment pools be further diversified through the employment of multiple investment managers and/or index funds, and . . . that the Regents oversee the management of the endowment funds through the establishment of investment goals and policy and the evaluation and selection of investment managers, rather than through such traditional means as the approval of individual investment transactions.*

As a clarification, then President Shapiro, a quantitative economist educated at Princeton,

> *wanted to assure himself and the Board that under whatever plan is developed only the Board can decide the level of risk to which the [portfolio] should be exposed with respect to the nature of income and payout requirements, total return objectives, asset allocation guidelines, manager acquisition criteria, and allocation of assets to particular managers. He asked if it was true that under this plan all those decisions would be reserved for the Board and only for the Board.*
>
> *Mr. Herbert [the Investment Officer] replied affirmatively.*

Of the investment policy issues listed by President Shapiro, the only one that has been fully retained by the Board of Regents today is "allocation of assets to particular managers."

Various other salient points of the discussion are worth noting. There was discussion of the Investment Office's estimate that the new approach would allow performance to improve by 2% per year over time. President Shapiro, in the spirit of the Efficient Market Hypothesis, remarked that

> *he does favor the multiple money manager concept, but he did not believe there was any magic to it. It would not be appropriate to anticipate that this move, independent of assuming any extra risk or giving up any extra liquidities, would give 200 basis points per year.*[4]

---

4   In 1973, Professor Burton Malkiel, another Princeton economist, had published *A Random Walk Down Wall Street,* bringing the Efficient Market Hypothesis to the

As a sign of the times, it was noted that "a number of institutions, along with the University, have been undertaking the diversification of assets and through that activity there is an introduction to diversification in management" and that it "appears that most large investment pools, such as major corporate pension funds, are shifting to multiple managers because they get an element of diversification and competition."

The search for new managers was undertaken with the assistance of the Wellesley Group (at that point called Investment Management Control Systems), investment consultants first engaged in 1978, and included an advertisement in the publication *Pensions & Investment Age*—now known as *Pensions & Investments*.

Thus although in prior years the University had only dabbled with additional managers in external fund vehicles, the policy of engaging multiple managers and moving away from approving individual transactions was now officially adopted by the Board of Regents. Under Michigan's Uniform Management of Institutional Funds Act (UMIFA), all this was now clearly legally permissible, as noted above.

In November 1986, the fundamental policy changes directed a year earlier were implemented. A lot happened! In the context of setting asset allocation and investment guidelines, the total return approach was now formally adopted for all endowment funds: Endowment funds should be managed, from both the investment return and distribution points of view, to seek to maintain, if not increase, the *real* value or "purchasing power" of the endowment. As discussed above, historically, the methodology both at the University and in the broader world had been the income approach—simply to distribute whatever income (interest and dividends) was in fact generated by the so-called corpus, or principal, of the fund. Instead, going forward, the University "needed . . . a distribution policy which will provide for enough reinvestment and appreciation to sustain the real value of the endowment over the long term."

The new approach was implicitly endorsed by UMIFA, which separated the concept of income from that of distributions. UMIFA implicitly recognized that

---

masses. In 1984, Warren Buffett gave a speech at Columbia University rebutting Malkiel's book and the Efficient Market Hypothesis. To date, according to Mr. Buffett, it seems Professor Malkiel has never responded. President Shapiro would have surely been familiar with Malkiel's book, but he might not have heard Buffett's speech.

there might be good reasons for a fund to distribute either *more* (selling invest-ments and distributing capital gains) or *less* (retaining income and reinvesting it) cash than the income it earned. This then represented the full adoption of the "Total Return Approach" across all portfolios.

For example, at the University of Michigan, in the 10 years ending June 30, 1986, with an annualized distribution averaging 6.8% to participants, the endowment had actually *lost* an annualized average of 2.7% in real value because returns had not kept up with inflation plus distributions. Thus one of the actions taken at this time was to set the payout rate for future distributions at 5.5% of the 3-year moving average market value (12 quarters).

On the return side, asset allocation was now focused on generating enough return to meet the distribution payout rate plus expected inflation—this required a heavily equity-oriented portfolio. The range of equities was set at 60% to 80% with a target of 70%; the rest would be fixed income—this represented a sig-nificant increase from the 1986 fiscal-year-end allocation of 47% to equities. Remember that a "Long-Term Objective" of a 45% allocation to equities had been set forth in a 1952 report 34 years before—long-term indeed!

Note that it appears that the concept from a few years earlier of *not* having asset allocation percentages for a total return portfolio had quietly disappeared.

In the context of diversification of managers—that is the multi-manager approach—it was recognized that going forward the Master List would be unworkable. So, finally, the Master List of Common Stocks was eliminated. Since there would be no Master List, no ratification by the Board of Regents of any changes to the Master List would be required. In addition, in order to respond to the new approach, instead of monthly reports of transactions for ratification, there would be newly developed quarterly reports, to include manager by man-ager statements of portfolio holdings, policies, and requirements: "Rather than details of individual transaction decisions, the Regents should be concerned with key statistics of performance and portfolio characteristics and analyses thereof," and the "changes alter the Regents' role with regard to endowment investment: they enhance Regental control at the policy level, while lessening Regental involvement at the transaction level."

With the help of the Wellesley Group, the 250 investment managers who had responded to the advertisement were divided into four groups according to the following investment styles: basic value, growth and income, growth, and aggres-sive growth. Because the designation of investment styles is to a degree arbitrary, it is interesting to note how investment styles were being thought about at this point in time. Of the 250 respondents, the following 6 managers were selected for the initial diversification:

Basic Value	Fidelity Management Trust Company
	Trinity Investment Management Corp.
Growth & Income	Boston Company
	Common Fund for South Africa Free Equity Investments
Growth	Atlanta/Sosnoff Capital Corp.
	Ariel Capital Management, Inc.
Aggressive Growth	None

It was projected that the number of separate stock issues held by the University would climb from a then current 66 to an estimated 300. Compare that with the number of *funds* held across portfolios as of June 30, 2016—well over 600! (see table on p. 76)

Equity managers "would be held to 150 basis points [after fees] over the Standard & Poor's 500 Stock Index"—apparently irrespective of individual investment style. Managers would be given a "three-year grace period in which to establish a performance history" during which they would generally not be dismissed. Performance would be measured over 3- to 5-year market cycles. Interestingly, guidelines related to "Stock Quality Ratings," although today considered outmoded in institutional equity management, were retained in November 1986: The average stock quality rating was to be "B+" (Average) or better, with some additional parameters. Standard & Poor's started publishing stock quality ratings in 1956 and continues publishing them to this day. The University stopped utilizing them 6 years later in July 1992.

For fixed income, the average quality would be maintained at "A" or better (investment grade), and "managers would be held to a standard of 100 basis points over the Shearson-Lehman Government/Corporate Bond Index."[5] Off the back of the inflationary/high interest rate period of the late 1970s and early 1980s, there was now an explicit recognition of the importance of not

---

5   In addition, "no bonds with a quality rating below an S&P 'BBB-'" could be held in the fixed-income portfolio. These guidelines for the fixed-income portfolio remain in place today, although they were somewhat relaxed in a November 1990 action, which allowed downgraded securities of up to 5% of the fixed-income portfolio to be held, though in no case for more than three years.

just credit risk but also *interest rate risk* in the management of a fixed-income portfolio.

For both fixed income and equity, it was recognized that "the greatly increased number of . . . holdings will provide diversification and tend to reduce overall portfolio risk"—in effect offsetting the risk of increased quality ranges.

As a result of the new multi-manager initiative, investment management fees were projected to increase from $300,000 to $1.2 million. However, it was also believed that "the projected improvement in performance would more than make up for the increase in cost." Consulting fees would remain unchanged.

Responding to the advent of take-over battles in corporate America, and in order to give the new managers clear guidance, the Board of Regents reaffirmed proxy policy, making it clear that proxies should be voted *against* management when the proposals (such as anti-takeover measures) were "detrimental to shareholders' voting rights and financial interests."

And finally, in November 1986, the Board of Regents approved the consolidation for investment purposes of the three major endowment funds into a single pool—what is now known as the University Endowment Fund (UEF). The consolidation was now permissible because *all* funds would now be managed on a total return basis, not just the pool of Funds Functioning as Endowment.

In November 1988, a Request for Action was approved that reflected the increasing sophistication of the financial markets, as well as that of the Investment Office. The Board of Regents authorized the use of "financial futures . . . in the management of the University's investments." A related Item for Information explained: "This is an example of the type of tool necessary to function effectively in the investment world today." Financial futures would be used in subsequent years in various ways to quickly and precisely manage and swap exposures, particularly in connection with currency, equity, and fixed-income "overlay" strategies.[6] Most immediately, as we describe next, financial futures would be used in connection with a new investment program, the Tactical Asset Allocation, or TAA, program.[7]

---

6 The use of futures had one additional advantage. For example, being long S&P 500 futures "would not involve ownership of stocks of companies with operations in South Africa" and thus would allow the endowment to achieve broader equity exposure than strictly permitted under the South African restrictions, which would remain in place until 1993.

7 The program was also sometimes referred to as "Strategic Asset Allocation."

The timing of the approval for the use of financial futures was not coincidental. The prior year had seen the dramatic and sudden "Black Monday" stock market crash of October 19, 1987, which resulted in a keen focus on risk management concepts and strategies. With this event providing the impetus, the Investment Office, at the same time it received this approval, embarked on a 10-year adventure with the TAA program. Grappling with how to safeguard the portfolio from future drawdowns, the Item for Information explained:

I believe very strongly—and my staff and the Wellesley Group support me in this—that traditional market timing is not the answer [to how to more actively manage asset allocation in the future]. There is a mountain of research to support our view that market timing is an extremely dangerous game. Some of that evidence was presented to the Board by the Wellesley Group in November 1986 and March 1987 and by Stanford Calderwood of Trinity Investment Management in March 1988. In particular, market timing by individuals, committees, and boards tend to be governed by emotion: fear drives us out of the market and greed keeps us in at precisely the wrong times. Such efforts are driven by a short-term perspective which is inappropriate in the management of an endowment fund whose horizon is, by definition, perpetual.

There is, however, a recently developed approach to market timing that appears worthy of consideration. It is a highly disciplined, quantitative approach relying on computerized manipulations of economic data rather than human judgment. This method relies on regression analyses of the comparative returns of stocks, bonds, and cash equivalents and other economic data such as indicators of liquidity and market momentum. Each manager who provides such a service has its own computer model which determines what the current weightings of each asset category should be.

Variously called strategic or tactical asset allocation, this approach can be implemented without the purchase and sale of individual securities and the associated delays, disruptions, and transactions costs. Instead, exposure to the various asset categories can be adjusted through the purchase and sale of financial futures as described in the Request for Action on financial futures.

The Request for Action further explained:

The Common Fund's second strategy utilizing futures is an asset allocation strategy. After conducting extensive back-tests and sponsoring a four year pilot program at Lawrence University, the Common Fund introduced their Strategic Asset Allocation

Program in 1986. . . . During the pilot program, Strategic Asset Allocation added about 4 percentage points per annum in performance. The results for the Common Fund's Equity Allocation Pool have been dramatic in the six quarters since its inception, returning 16.8 percent annualized versus 5.3 percent for the Standard & Poor's 500 as of June 30, 1988. Most of the added value came in the very unusual fourth quarter of 1987; these figures are not indicative of long-term performance expectations.

In fact, the Black Monday crash helped persuade the University to diversify more aggressively into private markets and illiquid alternatives, and decrease exposure to public markets.[8] The TAA program was seen as a way of reducing volatility in the portfolio while this diversification push was implemented. The first TAA program would be run by the Common Fund.

Despite the positive results during back-testing and the pilot, the TAA program did not work out well going forward. Already at the September 1990 meeting, it was noted that although the program was "conceptually not a timing strategy . . . its actual application often is." Performance was described as "extremely poor" and "miserable."[9] In October 1994, the University replaced the Common Fund TAA program with one run by First Quadrant, and in March 1998, the University discontinued the program entirely. The meeting minutes

---

8 Interestingly, at the January 1989 meeting, one Regent requested that some of the discussion relating to performance be "cited in the minutes as an extremely helpful way of dealing with the tendency of the Regents to use [a] short-run incident as an attack on long-term policy."

9 In a memorandum to the Regents dated October 1, 1990, following the market's reaction to the August invasion of Kuwait by Iraq and the poor performance of the TAA program, then CFO Farris Womack analyzed the general concept of quantitative modeling as follows:

As I have indicated to many of you, both publicly and privately, one of the difficulties I believe we are facing is the uncertainty of the applicability of the underlying models that investment managers are using. There are no econometric models that can forecast a major upheaval in the world's political situation and there are certainly none that would predict the kind of aggression that occurred in Kuwait. Perhaps even more important than the uncertainties associated with that are those associated with the resulting disequilibrium caused by the run-up in other commodities and especially the uncertainty of oil. Models are based on conditions which have obtained over time. The estimates obtained from such models are always necessarily limited when any of the major components fall outside the range of predictability. That is precisely the case that has occurred with oil.

noted that "exposure to tactical asset allocation also hurt performance in 1997" and "now that the portfolio has been well diversified with the corresponding decrease in risk, there is no longer a need for this program."

The June 1989 meeting continued, though with significant debate, the expansion into alternative assets. Cambridge Associates, which had recently been engaged as outside consultant in addition to the Wellesley Group and remains the University's primary investment consultant to this day, made a presentation to the Board of Regents recommending further diversification of endowment funds into the following alternative asset classes: (i) a 5% allocation to oil and gas investments, (ii) a 5% allocation to venture capital, and (iii) a $10 million allocation to "reorganization" investments—which currently are more commonly called "distressed" investments. The proposal for reorganization investments was stated as a fixed dollar amount rather than as a percentage because the opportunity was seen as a temporary one.

The oil and gas and venture capital investments would form part of the equity allocation of 70%, and the reorganization investments would fall into the fixed-income allocation of 30%—although reorganization or distressed investments would later be reclassified as equity.

The master plan was to "further diversify the assets of the University Endowment Fund to decrease the fund's exposure to the traditional, domestic, high capitalization, high quality publicly-traded stocks and bonds. Our goal is to dampen the volatility of endowment returns." It was explained that the three asset classes themselves had quite different characteristics, furthering the objective of diversification. The oil and gas investment in particular could provide "a reliable hedge against inflation." Venture capital funds might have a life of "ten to fifteen years."

These new asset classes had "in common a lack of liquidity." But the University was the type of long-term investor that could bear less liquidity and be rewarded with higher returns—"in the range of 20 to 30 percent historically."

Even though a study of the endowments of 380 institutions demonstrated that the "University's performance was behind that of the average of the other institutional endowments and that its endowment fund was allocated differently," some Regents treaded hesitantly in the new waters. One Regent sought an opinion of counsel as to whether the proposed investments "would meet the prudent man standard of trust investment"—although at this point in time, as discussed above, UMIFA governed in Michigan, not the law of trusts. Another Regent was concerned that the proposed investments were "very risky and highly speculative, and therefore would not be prudent and would not demonstrate good stewardship." However, another Regent observed, noting the University's underperformance and with a nod to Modern Portfolio Theory, that "it can be just as imprudent not to add a category of investment as it is to add it."

In the end, the Board of Regents deferred a decision on the venture capital and oil and gas proposals, focusing strictly on the reorganization investment proposal for which the University needed an immediate answer. The Board of Regents did approve this investment, with two Regents dissenting, but subject to a dollar cap of $3 million and the investments being in "secured debt."

There was an important proposal from the administration regarding governance that was raised in the Request for Action from June 1989:

> We further recommend that specific investments within each category be made with the approval of the Vice President and Chief Financial Officer.
>
> Admittedly, this approach is a new one. The meeting schedule of the Board does not always permit timely consideration of specific opportunities. Moreover, if we are to take greater initiative in seeking out investment opportunities, it may no longer be appropriate to ask for the Board's consideration of each individual fund. Rather, it may be necessary for the Board to take more of a "macro-management" approach in order to best provide its fiduciary oversight.

Here we see the administration already thinking through the mechanics of how investing in new funds would work from an approvals point of view. The CFO (and presumably the Investment Officer) reasonably considered that to best provide "fiduciary oversight" it might make sense for the Board of Regents *not* to approve each individual investment opportunity, but rather that it might make more sense for the Board to focus on higher level portfolio issues such as overall asset allocation. The administration also foresaw the timing issues that could arise with respect to new investment opportunities—issues with which the Investment Office grapples to this day.

As we will shortly see, in the end, this approach was *not* adopted at this time. One might surmise that this entire business of illiquid alternatives investing and the engagement of multiple managers in strange new asset classes was just too novel and untested for the Board of Regents to become fully comfortable, at least at this moment, with fully delegating manager engagements to the administration.

December 1989 revisited and crystallized the issues brought up in June. Proposed asset allocations for all asset classes were set forth—in effect a full Model Portfolio, although the percentages were still regarded as more limits than targets. As in June, oil and gas, and venture capital, were each proposed at 5%—but now they were also approved. Reorganization investments were now given an allocation of 2.5% (not just a fixed dollar amount), and real estate was added at 10%. Overall equity/fixed income remained targeted at 70%/30%.

A four-page "Statement of Objectives and Guidelines for the Management of Alternative Asset Classes" (Alternative Asset Guidelines), prepared with the assistance of Cambridge Associates, was attached to the December 1989 Request for Action. Many of the principles set forth in this document are still observed today. It is interesting to note that the Alternative Asset Guidelines lists the diversification into "asset classes that have a low statistical correlation with the stock market" and the reduction of volatility as the "Primary Objectives" of alternative assets, with the enhancement of return listed as a "Secondary Objective." Presumably this was part of the continuing effort to convince certain Regents that although a particular alternative investment might appear overly risky when taken solely on its own, it could nonetheless still be appropriate, and even recommendable, as part of a large and diversified portfolio of assets with varied risk levels. Nonetheless, with respect to the proposed allocations, the then CFO apparently still felt compelled to emphasize at the Board of Regents meeting that "these are the absolute maximum percentages that would apply at any one time; it is unlikely that the University would ever obtain that degree of exposure"—a statement, we note, that was not consistent with what was set forth in the actual Request for Action.

Importantly, the administration made a new governance proposal:

> *While the earlier Request for Action proposed that specific investment vehicles be selected with the approval of the Vice President and Chief Financial Officer, in this Item we recommend that individual investment vehicles be brought to the Board for approval.*

This then is the genesis for the process still in place today, whereby the Investment Office seeks Regental approval for new managers. At the time, the proposed process made sense, since investing in alternative assets and private partnerships was a relatively new and untested initiative, and the number of managers was limited. However, already the plan was to increase the number: "In general, this type of diversification into several funds is the model of investing envisioned for all alternative asset classes."

In accordance with the new process, the Investment Office sought approval for three new partnership investments—one oil and gas, one venture capital, and an additional reorganization investment with a different manager than the one approved in June.

CHAPTER FOUR

The 1990s
The "Endowment Model" Matures

As can be seen from the chart on p. 3, in the 1990s, various factors conspired to produce unprecedented growth in the real value of the endowment. One was an increasing allocation to equities coupled with strong investment returns in the U.S. bull market of the '90s. Another was, as discussed above, that starting in 1987 the endowment payout had been recalibrated to protect the real value of the endowment. And finally, the University's Development Office launched its first truly massive campaign, the "Billion Dollar Campaign for Michigan." The Regental resolution approving this campaign noted that it would be "the largest fundraising campaign in the history of the institution, indeed the largest fundraising campaign ever undertaken by a public university." On the next page is a chart highlighting all the major fundraising campaigns at the University of Michigan, including the Billion Dollar Campaign for Michigan:[1]

During the 1990s, the University aggressively implemented the new policy directions of the late 1980s by expanding heavily into alternative investments and new alternative asset classes; engaging many new managers; investing in commodities, financial futures, and more internationally; and adapting processes and reports as a result.

---

1   The "Development Council," the predecessor to the Development Office, was first established as a "fund-raising unit" in August 1951. In October 1969, the permanent staff in the "central fund-raising office" was renamed "Development Office."

Impact of Campaigns

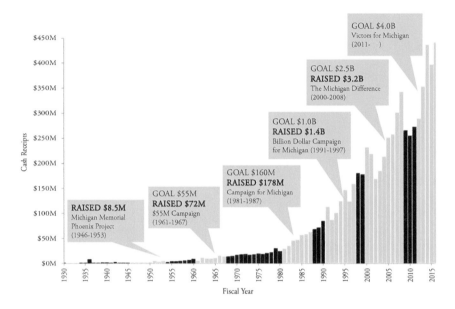

An important development took place in January 1990. As described in greater detail in a separate section below, then Vice President and Chief Financial Officer Farris Womack formed the Investment Advisory Committee (IAC), which held its first meeting. Through the 1990s and beyond, the IAC would be instrumental in advising and supporting the University's investment program in its push to diversify into different asset classes, particularly into new alternative asset classes. The different IAC members, each a prominent investment professional with experience in different areas, would contribute their general as well as specialized expertise.

In August 1991, the University moved the custody of its assets from National Bank of Detroit to The Boston Safe Deposit & Trust Company, later acquired by a predecessor of BNY Mellon, the University's current custodian. The University needed a new custodian with the capabilities to handle the developing complexities of its growing portfolios.

In April 1992, the investment-related Bylaws were tweaked to add the "associate vice president for finance" as a permissible signatory.

In July 1992, with the recommendation of Cambridge Associates and the support of the IAC, the Board of Regents terminated the use of "stock quality rating restrictions which may interfere with [managers'] management styles or with their ability to take advantage of market options."[2]

In October 1992, asset- and mortgage-backed securities were approved. It is interesting that it was determined necessary to secure this approval, since historically the University had, as we have seen, been heavily invested directly in mortgages and contracts secured by land. Nonetheless, it seems that by October 1992 the "University's internally managed funds do not presently contain any publicly traded asset-backed or mortgage-backed fixed income securities." So presumably it was deemed conservative to obtain the approval—to be fair, these new types of securities were not the same instruments as the mortgages and contracts of old.

The University's investment program had to keep pace with the growth in funds under management, and it did. By February 1993, the University had investments with 10 different venture capital funds. It was in this month that the Board of Regents approved the first commitment to a "private equity" fund: $10 million to Welsh, Carson, Anderson & Stowe VI, L.P.

In April 1993, finally implementing a change that seems to have been approved back in November 1986, the Board of Regents amended the Bylaws relating to investing, this time to implement "the replacement of the monthly Report of Investment Transactions with the new comprehensive investment report." Thus the Investment Office finally stopped reporting individual investment transactions to the Board of Regents, but a new investment report would be required to "allow the Regents to monitor compliance with the guidelines being adopted." These changes reflected the growing importance of asset allocation decisions, manager selection, and the investment in funds—versus security selection and individual transactions—in the evolution of investing at the University.

In fact, what is now the "Private Equity" asset class developed as an outgrowth of the University's venture capital investment program. In February 1994, the Board of Regents approved a second private equity investment (still under the venture capital rubric): $5 million to WPG Corporate Development Associates IV, L.P., to "focus on middle-market buyouts, an area in which we have not

---

2   IAC members shared a common sentiment which was succinctly expressed in the notes of the June 19, 1992 meeting as follows: "Ira Harris said that by imposing such guidelines, we are hiring managers but having Standard & Poor's decide our investments."

previously invested." The Request for Action made it clear that the fund would not be involved with "the highly leveraged hostile takeovers which were highly publicized in the eighties." Private equity investments continued to be added to the venture capital portfolio.

April 1994 brought important structural changes to the University's investments. The "University Investment Pool" (UIP), the term that was—and still occasionally is—used for the University's working capital funds, had grown to well over $900 million and was invested primarily in highly liquid short- to intermediate-maturity fixed-income securities and funds. *Not* investing these assets more aggressively for the long term represented a significant opportunity cost to the University. Because the University did not have, at this point, the need for this much actual working capital, it was determined that a "permanent core" of these assets, initially set to be $700 million, could and should be invested in endowment-type investments. So it was at this time that the "Long Term Portfolio" (LTP) was created (and is still in existence today) as a unitized portfolio whose primary owners would be the University Endowment Fund (UEF)—representing the existing endowment funds—and the UIP.[3] The plan was to transition assets over a 3- to 5-year period. "Financial futures and other derivatives would be used, as appropriate, to facilitate the transition." It was made clear that the "investment objective for the University Investment Pool will be to maximize total return, not just yield. Accordingly, UIP's investment performance will be measured on a total return basis."

These new funds, along with new funds flowing in from the Billion Dollar Campaign for Michigan, would keep the Investment Office busy making new alternative asset commitments. As a result of this increased activity, it soon became clear that the potential problems with the alternative asset approvals process that had been anticipated by the Investment Office in June 1989 had in fact materialized: In certain situations, the Investment Office was not able to obtain timely Regental approvals.

---

3   The UIP investment in the endowment did not represent the investment of a "true" endowment and therefore was made under the rubric of "Funds Functioning as Endowment," discussed previously. Funds Functioning as Endowment were later (and are now) more commonly called "quasi-endowments." Because of the University's management of funds other than "true" endowments, a provision in the Michigan constitution limiting equity investment by the University to the "endowment" has necessitated considerable legal analysis.

A Request for Action introduced in May 1994 explained:

In certain cases when early funds have been very successful, interests in new funds are offered only to existing investors, who must react very quickly if they want to increase their participation over previous fund levels.

. . .

. . . This type of timetable is not unusual for groups of this stature.

. . . the general partner decided to cut back allocations of all investors who had not yet received final approval for their commitments. Due to the Regental calendar, the University of Michigan was one of the investors who was cut back.

If we have chosen our general partners well, we will encounter these problems more and more frequently in the future.

Thus the May 1994 item requested that "follow-on investments"—that is, investments in a fund sponsored by the *same* management group with "essentially the same strategy and core investment personnel"—no longer required Board of Regents approval, but rather only the approval of two University officers. The Investment Office would, however, still *notify* the Board of Regents of these follow-on investments. Other alternative asset investments, principally consisting of investments with *new* management groups, would still be brought to the Board of Regents for approval.[4] This is the process still in place today.

Just 4 months later, in September 1994, there was another important revision to policy. This revision was similarly driven by the new inflows of cash, the rapid pace of investing and growth of the alternatives portfolio, and the fact that alternatives partnerships can have unpredictable cash drawdowns on their commitments, as well as unpredictable distributions. The Investment Office requested greater flexibility by eliminating the alternatives subclass *limits,* instead replacing the limits with *one overall target* for alternative assets: 25% of the portfolio. This percentage now also included the category of "alternative fixed income investments" (a category that included the reorganization investments) that were in this same Request for Action, reclassified out of the general fixed-income asset class into the general equities asset class, due to their equity-like characteristics.

---

4   In addition, increasing the originally approved commitment amount by up to 10% in a fund with a new manager (termed an "add-on investment") would also not require Regental approval.

Finally, paralleling this last reclassification, the "target asset allocation"[5] was modified to 75% equity and 25% fixed income—moving 5% from fixed income to equity.

In June 1995, in order to help protect the long-term real value of the endowment, the University brought down the distribution rate from the very first fixed rate of 5.5% set in November 1986 to 5%. The change would be implemented gradually over a 5-year period.

In July 1996, the overall "target asset allocation" was again changed: Equity was increased further to 80% (range: 65% to 85%) and fixed income lowered to 20% (range: 15% to 35%). The change was justified by the fact that the equity side of the portfolio (which included alternatives) was becoming highly diversified across different asset classes, and thus "equity" risk was mitigated. In addition, in the same Request for Action, the Board of Regents first approved investments in commodities. Commodities would be viewed as an alternative asset, and the target level for alternative assets was raised from 25% to 30%.

The December 1997 Report of Investments (ROI) changed the name of the entire venture capital asset class to the broader "Private Equity," recognizing that the allocation had become more than just venture investing. This was short-lived. In the very next ROI (June 1999),[6] the asset classes were, logically, broken into two—Private Equity and Venture Capital—and would remain that way through today.

In September 1998, after years of discussion at IAC meetings, the Board of Regents approved four separate $25 million investments with "Absolute Return Managers."[7] This was a new asset class. The Request for Action explained:

---

5   Currently, the "Model Portfolio" construct is used—which *does* contain targets by subasset classes. Once the alternatives asset class had matured and the endowment value had grown, actual allocation percentages were more stable, and it became reasonable to separately target allocations for each of the alternative subasset classes, such as real estate, venture capital, oil and gas (now called Natural Resources), and so on. There is still, nonetheless, an overall minimum set for Fixed Income of 10% per a February 2006 item.

6   As explained in the section "Periodic Reports to the Regents," there were no Reports of Investments published in 1998.

7   The minutes for the December 6, 1994 IAC meeting noted that David Thurston of Cambridge Associates had suggested that an appropriate target for hedge fund investments (a narrower term for absolute return) was 700 b.p. over the S&P 500—quite aggressive by today's standards!

The term "absolute return" describes investment strategies whose objective is to produce positive returns in all types of markets. These strategies attempt to produce returns more dependent upon manager skill than on the direction of the capital markets. Thus, a traditional investment manager is evaluated on a relative basis compared with the appropriate market index, while an absolute return manager is evaluated against an absolute *return standard.*

Although the Request for Action explained that the University had in effect already been investing in the Absolute Return asset class through its distressed debt funds (as reorganization investments were now called) as well as its emerging market and energy long/short stock funds, the proposed investments nonetheless represented a big step. But the concept of investing in absolute return was prescient—U.S. and world markets were closing in on all-time highs. The Absolute Return asset class would include funds that are commonly called "hedge funds."

With the addition of the Absolute Return asset class, the asset allocation chart in the June 1999 ROI took on the basic form and categories of investment that it maintains today—although distressed debt was not yet part of the Absolute Return asset class.

The millennium ended with a consideration of the only divestment initiative, other than South African Apartheid, that has been adopted by the Board of Regents. In March 1999, the Board of Regents formed the requisite ad hoc advisory committee to consider the divestment of "securities issued by tobacco companies." In June 2000, following the recommendation of the ad hoc advisory committee, the Board of Regents voted to divest. One Regent noted: "The University's position as a premier institution in health education and health research, and as a health care provider, dictates a yes vote."[8]

---

8   The policy on considering divestment initiatives was memorialized and further explained in a November 17, 2005 statement by then Executive Vice President and Chief Financial Officer Timothy P. Slottow. A related discussion held at the November 2005 Regents meeting is further instructive.

CHAPTER FIVE

2000 Through Today
The Chief Investment Office

In September 1999, "in light of the growing complexity and size of the University's investment portfolios, and as part of our continuing evolution of the University's endowment management," the University established the Chief Investment Office (the "Office of the Chief Investment Officer") as a unit separate from the Treasurer's Office and created the position of Chief Investment Officer (CIO), now reporting directly to the Executive Vice President and Chief Financial Officer. This action was a true milestone in the history of the Investment Office—the growing complexity and size of the investment portfolios was thus reflected in the growing importance and stature of the Investment Office. L. Erik Lundberg was appointed as the first (and remains the current) CIO, although he would be the fifth Investment Officer since Julius Schmidt was first appointed in 1931.

From 2000 onward, building on the structural changes of the preceding two decades, the number of managers and funds in all asset classes increased and the portfolio became ever more diversified. Although *absolute* returns decreased somewhat relative to the 1990s, returns *relative* to the total return of the S&P 500 index improved considerably, as can be seen in the following chart.[1]

---

1   This chart is for illustrative purposes only. During this lengthy time period, the endowment portfolio changed in composition over time and had different characteristics than the S&P 500, including having significant allocations to fixed income (particularly earlier

Endowment vs S&P 500 Total Return Index
Rolling 10-Year Annualized Returns

In 2000, David Swensen, CIO at Yale University, published *Pioneering Portfolio Management,* a landmark in the history of the now commonly called "Endowment Model" of investing. The Endowment Model relies heavily on illiquid alternatives and on astute and creative strategy and manager selection. It was de facto being developed and implemented simultaneously at numerous endowments starting in the 1980s, including, as we've seen, at the University of Michigan.

By the time the new Chief Investment Office was established, the asset classifications of the primary endowment pool, the Long Term Portfolio, were fairly settled. Now the Model Portfolio became the starting point of asset allocation, benchmarking, performance reporting, and the Investment Office Incentive Plan. The following table traces how the Model Portfolio allocations changed over this time period. The first column for each year after 2000 is the change from the prior Model Portfolio (e.g., the 44% model Equities

---

on), greater diversification generally, less volatility, and later on, less liquidity due to the growth in illiquid alternatives asset classes.

allocation in 2004 was 5% less than it was in 2000). Note that the Model Portfolio was only adjusted in the specific years listed:

CHANGES IN LTP MODEL ASSET ALLOCATIONS (%)								
	2000	2004		2007		2009		2014
Equities	49	–5	44	–4	40	–5	35	–5	30
Fixed Income	18	NC	18	–3	15	–3	12	NC	12
Cash	0	NC	0	NC	+0	NC	0	+3	3
Absolute Return	10	+5	15	NC	15	+1	16	–1	15
Venture Capital	7	–2	5	–1	4	+1	5	+3	8
Private Equity	7	NC	7	+3	10	+2	12	NC	12
Real Estate	6	+1	7	+3	10	+2	12	NC	12
Natural Res.	3	+1	4	+2	6	+2	8	NC	8

The next table, for the same years, traces the changes in the actual portfolio:

CHANGES IN LTP ACTUAL ASSET ALLOCATIONS (%)								
	2000	2004		2007		2009		2014
Equities	34.2	+7.0	41.2	–8.4	32.8	–8.0	24.8	+2.7	27.5
Fixed Income	18.7	–3.1	15.6	–5.9	9.7	+0.1	9.8	–2.8	7.0
Cash	0.9	–0.4	0.5	+1.1	1.6	–0.7	0.9	+3.9	4.8
Absolute Return	9.7	+10.8	20.5	+0.3	20.8	–0.3	20.5	–6.6	13.9
Venture Capital	20.7	–17.3	3.4	+2.2	5.6	+2.1	7.7	+4.4	12.1
Private Equity	6.2	0.2	6.4	+5.1	11.5	+2.2	13.7	NC	13.7
Real Estate	6.3	+0.7	7.0	+3.7	10.7	+1.6	12.3	+0.3	12.6
Natural Res.	3.3	+2.1	5.4	+1.9	7.3	+3.0	10.3	–1.9	8.4

The final table, for the same years, shows the difference between the model and actual portfolios (e.g., the actual 2004 Equities allocation was 14.8% less than the model allocation):

DIFFERENCE BETWEEN LTP ACTUAL AND MODEL ASSET ALLOCATIONS (%)

	2000	2004	2007	2009	2014
Equities	−14.8	−2.8	−7.2	−10.2	−2.5
Fixed Income	+0.7	−2.4	−5.3	−2.2	−5.0
Cash	+0.9	+0.5	+1.6	+0.9	+1.8
Absolute Return	−0.3	+5.5	+5.8	+4.5	−1.1
Venture Capital	+13.7	−1.6	+1.6	+2.7	+4.1
Private Equity	−0.8	−0.6	+1.5	+1.7	+1.7
Real Estate	+0.3	NC	+0.7	+0.3	+0.6
Natural Res.	+0.3	+1.4	+1.3	+2.3	+0.4

In March 2001, the Board of Regents approved an item that confirmed the authority of the Executive Vice President and CFO to designate "Funds Functioning as Endowment," commonly termed "quasi-endowment." Above, we described how the construct of Funds Functioning as Endowment was first introduced in December 1969 and how in April 1994 a "permanent core" of the University's working capital/nonrestricted funds was designated as Funds Functioning as Endowment. In addition to confirming and clarifying the CFO's authority in this area, the item made clear that such funds should generally be "locked-up" for a minimum of 5 years:

> Funds functioning as endowment generally consist of institutional funds the expenditure of the principal of which is not restricted by external instruments, but which the institution has determined to hold and invest as long term capital and as part of the institution's endowment.
>
> . . . .
>
> Designations of funds as funds functioning as endowment may be permanent or for a term of years, generally not less than five, subject in either case to the ability of the Executive Vice President and Chief Financial Officer to expend principal of the funds in exigent circumstance resulting from unanticipated reductions in revenues or increases in expenses, as shall be determined by the Executive Vice President and Chief Financial Officer.

The University of Michigan, including its Investment Office, has always been subject to the State of Michigan's Freedom of Information Act (FOIA) statute.

Historically, FOIA was not a concern for the Investment Office. Then, beginning in 2002, financial information vendors, interested for commercial purposes particularly in the returns of prominent venture capital investment managers, began availing themselves of the statute and requesting detailed information about the University's portfolio. This created deep concern with numerous investment managers, particularly certain prominent venture capital firms—even to the point of refusing to permit the University to continue investing with them. The University's investment program was seriously threatened. The new CIO and Investment Office staff took action and ultimately persuaded the University to seek an amendment from the Michigan legislature to a related protective statute. In 2004, the statute was amended, becoming the Confidential Research and Investment Information Act (CRIIA). The new CRIIA largely resolved the issue, although the Investment Office is still routinely called upon to give comfort and provide detailed explanations of the University's FOIA/CRIIA situation to concerned investment managers.

In June 2006, the distribution policy, last changed in June 1995, was revisited. In order to give even greater stability to the amount of the payout, the averaging period was extended from 12 quarters (3 years) to 28 quarters (7 years)—and once again, this was implemented gradually. In July 2010, as had been contemplated as early as 1995, in order to preserve the long-term purchasing power of the endowment, the University again brought down the distribution rate, this time from 5% to 4.5%. This change was also implemented gradually.

In December 2006, as part of the approval of the SGAM/4D Global Energy Development Capital Fund II for the Natural Resources portfolio (then called the "Energy" portfolio), the Board of Regents also approved

> *up to an additional $10 million commitment to be used for co-investment opportunities which will be offered to the limited partners to the extent that a partnership acquisition exceeds investment limitations. These co-investment opportunities are expected to be at more attractive terms than the Fund investment.*

This is the first time the University sought approval for co-investment opportunities, and the quoted language from the item itself highlighted two typical characteristics of co-investments: (i) they tend to involve special situations with larger transaction amounts than are appropriate for the main fund and (ii) they tend to involve better economics in terms of management fees than apply in the main fund. In fact, in February 2008, pursuant to this approval, the University made its first co-investment in Fairfield Energy Limited, developing oil and gas assets in the North Sea.

In 2009, the State of Michigan adopted the Uniform Prudent Management of Institutional Funds Act (UPMIFA), a modernization of (and replacement for) UMIFA, which had been adopted 33 years prior (see Appendix Exhibit A1, pp. 77–80). The revisions in UPMIFA were mostly incremental, in contrast to the sea change represented by the adoption of the Prudent Investor Rule and the elimination of legal lists discussed above. Nonetheless, the revisions were valuable. For example, recognizing the widespread use of external investment managers by charitable institutions, UPMIFA specified in greater detail the authority of an institution to delegate "to an external agent the management and investment of an institutional fund."

In December 2011, the Board of Regents approved a unique new venture capital investment program—termed Michigan Investment in New Technology Startups, or MINTS. These guidelines were amended technically in July 2013. MINTS co-invests with professional venture capital firms in start-ups whose business is based on intellectual property licensed through the University's Office of Technology Transfer. The program is part of the broader venture capital allocation of the endowment portfolio, the LTP, and importantly supports the University's technology commercialization efforts. Although small relative to the entire endowment, the program is significant in that it appears to be the first time that the University's endowment was authorized to *directly* invest in the equity of *private* companies—that said, it does somewhat represent a return to the *direct* (albeit *public*) investing that prevailed in the past.[2]

MINTS can be viewed as a late-stage step in the maturation of the technology transfer process in research institutions that began with the passage of the Bayh-Dole Act in 1980. The Bayh-Dole Act amended intellectual property law to allow universities to pursue ownership of inventions made using federal funding—previously these had to be assigned to the federal government. As of June 30, 2016, the

---

2   It is interesting to note that as early as February 1991, Al Taubman, then on the University's IAC (in addition, of course, to being a major donor), presciently suggested, as reflected in the meeting notes, that "the University invest in venture capital ideas originating with its own faculty."

University had invested in 19 MINTS startups, commercializing inventions both in the biomedical area and in various engineering fields.

In December 2013, the Board of Regents approved a special investment delegation giving the Executive Vice President and CFO "the authority to approve up to two new investment managers or vehicles" without, at that moment, setting forth what the potential investment or investments were. This delegation was requested for two related reasons. The first had to do with the Regental calendar and the need to potentially have to close the investment, the terms of which had still not been fully established, before it could be approved by the Board of Regents. The second had to do with confidentiality: Given the public nature of the Regental approval process, the University was not in a position to disclose any specifics, or even the existence, of a potential transaction due to confidentiality restrictions. In the end, the $69 million investment, code-named "Project Ranger," was in fact completed and represented—outside of MINTS—the first time the University would make a direct and independent private investment. The opportunity was brought to the University by Sam Zell, a long-standing donor and friend of the University, and involved purchasing a portfolio of life insurance policies together with other partners.

In August 2014, the Investment Office executed its first ever "secondary sale": approximately $355 million worth of real estate partnerships. It was a structure with partially deferred payments and negotiated credit protections. Typically, illiquid partnership interests are not sold, but rather are held through liquidation. In this case, the Investment Office was able to take advantage of favorable market conditions to rebalance its real estate asset allocation, as well as streamline the number of manager relationships it maintained in this asset class.

CHAPTER SIX

A Short History of
Benchmarking at the University

As was mentioned above, the advent and widespread implementation of benchmarking has changed the investment industry. In the early days, before the adoption of total return investing, the focus was on earned (and distributed) income, and market values were relatively unimportant. This manner of viewing investing was not as conducive to benchmarking as the total return approach, so in these early days benchmarking in general had not been widely adopted by the investment industry. Not surprisingly then, there were no mentions of benchmarking in early University of Michigan records.

At Michigan, total return investing was first adopted for a portion of the portfolio in 1970, and only fully adopted in November 1986 (see above). But starting with the 1980 Report of Investments (ROI), references to various types of benchmarks and benchmarking began to appear.

In fact, from 1980 through the creation of the Chief Investment Office in 1999, arguably the principal "benchmark" for the endowment was not called a "benchmark" but a "goal": "for total return to exceed inflation[1] plus distributions." If performance exceeded this goal and the endowment thus grew in real

---

[1] The inflation measure that was used during this time period was the CPI, published by the U.S. government. Currently, a measure called the Higher Education Price Index (HEPI), published by the National Association of College and University Business Officers (NACUBO), is utilized instead. HEPI is constructed to better and more directly capture the change in costs at institutions of higher learning than the CPI.

terms, all the better. Although certainly this metric continues to be an important one to consider, particularly as a long-term target, it does not serve well as a benchmark to judge the performance of investment managers and of an investment office. One, it provides no relative reference as to how the portfolio and its managers have performed given market conditions in different asset classes. Two, in a way, it puts the cart before the horse because the distribution policy itself should ultimately be a function of the returns the endowment has achieved, and is reasonably expected to achieve (with appropriate levels of risk), not the other way around. This is consistent with the University's approach starting in June 1986, when the University began adjusting distribution policy in accordance with conservative estimates of future returns.

In the December 1980 ROI, there was a table comparing the returns of the endowment portfolios under "Fixed Income" to the "Salomon Brothers Bond Index" and a reference to comparing returns under "Common Stocks" to the "Standard and Poor's 500"—one of the earliest references to benchmarking against published indices.

The June 1986 ROI[2] contained an early reference to the "Endowment and Foundation Index"—then an index of 76 endowment and foundation funds. This is the first reference to a peer-performance index that we found, against which the University could compare its own performance.[3]

The December 1986 ROI contained for the first time "Objectives for Equity and Fixed Income Investment Managers"—targeted benchmarking for the underlying managers themselves. The objective for equity managers was to outperform the S&P 500 by a "minimum of 1.5 percentage points . . . measured over three- to five-year periods of time to generally correspond with market cycles." Fixed-income managers were targeted to outperform the Shearson-Lehman Government/Corporate Bond Index by a minimum of 1% over the same periods.

The June 1987 ROI referenced the first blended total fund performance benchmark—in this case a "70/30 Index" composed of the S&P 500 and the Shearson-Lehman Government/Corporate Bond Index.

---

2   Driving home the concept that the inflation-plus-distributions "goal" does not constitute a good benchmark, this ROI states: "While the performance of the endowment funds relative to inflation is encouraging, comparisons of their recent performance with the Endowment and Foundation Index show they might have done better."

3   The first reference to "quartile" performance against peers we found in an ROI was in the June 1999 ROI.

The December 1987 ROI aggressively expanded references to various indices in numerous parts of the report. A number of indices were new to the report—such as the Wilshire 5000 and the NASDAQ Composite.

The ROIs in the 1990s further expanded the references to benchmarks and indices—including starting to add benchmarks and indices for alternative assets. The December 1997 ROI already noted: "Unfortunately, good time-weighted benchmarks are not available for all of the asset classes in which we invest." This is a perennial issue for institutional investors even today.

With the establishment of the Chief Investment Office in 1999, benchmarking was on its way to taking its current general form, sophistication, and importance. The Investment Office currently primarily uses two carefully constructed benchmarks, the "Custom Benchmark" and the "Blended Passive Benchmark."

The Custom Benchmark applies individual benchmarks to the different asset classes and rolls them up at Model Portfolio weights. The individual benchmarks for the shorter-term 1- and 3-year evaluation periods versus the longer-term 5- and 10-year periods can be different for the same asset class (which happens typically for alternatives asset classes). The reason is that the shorter period benchmarks are used more to evaluate Investment Office performance in terms of asset allocation and manager selection, while the longer period benchmarks are used more to evaluate whether a sufficient illiquidity premium is being achieved over the long term versus comparable liquid public markets.

The Blended Passive Benchmark is a benchmark composed of only liquid indices, which can be used to compare the actively managed endowment's returns over the very long term to what a completely passive (and liquid) investment program might have achieved.

Finally, we note that it appears from the record that the Board of Regents of the University of Michigan has never been involved in the selection or structuring of benchmarks, although, as described below, the IAC has.

CHAPTER SEVEN

The Investment Advisory Committee

M any endowments have outside investment advisory committees that meet periodically and assist the institution in the investment of its assets, but whose specific roles and responsibilities can vary widely. The University of Michigan has such a group, called the "Investment Advisory Committee" or IAC. Like many other such groups, Michigan's IAC has consisted principally of prominent investment professionals that have some historical affiliation with the University—whether as alumni, donors, or in some other capacity.

The University's IAC was formed by then Vice President and Chief Financial Officer (CFO) Farris W. Womack in January 1990. The first three members of the IAC were David W. Belin, J. Ira Harris, and A. Alfred Taubman. Although at this time James Duderstadt was President of the University of Michigan, Mr. Belin and Mr. Harris had begun discussing the formation of an investment advisory committee with the prior President, Harold Shapiro, some years earlier. Mr. Belin's and Mr. Harris' recommendations were part of their encouragement to optimize investment performance and continue modernizing the University's investment model in order to, among other things, better attract donations from alumni and others. The idea being that, without outstanding performance, donors might be less inclined to entrust monies to the University's management.

The first meeting was held at the Oxford Conference Center in Ann Arbor on February 8, 1990, and was a great success. The CFO sent letters to each of the members, thanking them for their participation. The tone was patently enthusiastic about the value of the IAC. As he wrote to one member, "I am convinced after this one session that the performance of the University's endowment will be enhanced significantly by your participation and each of us here looks forward to future discussions."

The second meeting took place on May 31, 1990, also in Ann Arbor, and already the format began taking on its current form: Three Regents joined the meeting and a representative of Cambridge Associates played an active role, all in addition to the IAC members themselves, the CFO, and Investment Office staff. Also, Terrence A. Elkes had become the fourth member of the IAC. In an exception to the current format, for the first few years meetings were actually held *three* times per year, before transitioning to the current two.

At the December 1991 IAC meeting, a new member joined, Sanford R. Robertson, bringing the total members of the IAC to five. Mr. Robertson would play a crucial role in providing introductions to prominent venture capital firms, thus helping build the University's venture capital program.

As a group, the IAC has given advice and support on a range of matters, focusing on (i) general investment strategy, asset allocation, and the model portfolio; (ii) new manager introductions and approvals; (iii) ongoing manager relationships; (iv) benchmarks; and (v) spending policy, as well as on some University issues that are not strictly investment related.

The IAC meeting format has broadly been the same, with members of the investment team, the CFO, up to three Regents, and a representative from the consultant Cambridge Associates attending. In later years, the President would sometimes attend part of the meeting. In addition, members of the IAC have been available on an ad hoc basis for individual consultations.

As a memorandum from Farris Womack dated November 15, 1995 noted: "The committee is advisory to the Executive Vice President/Chief Financial Officer; it has no official standing and makes no decisions. Its purpose is to provide for the intelligent, informed, and thorough discussion of investment issues."

At the end of 1996, Farris Womack stepped down as the University's CFO, and it appears that no formal IAC meetings were held from 1997 through 1999.

In the year 2000, following the establishment of a separate Chief Investment Office, the IAC was reconstituted, and the committee and meetings fully took on their current format. Membership was increased (currently to nine members), the consultant Cambridge Associates played a less active role, the Investment Office began preparing its own IAC materials, and there was less emphasis on discussing existing or proposed individual managers. Finally, the current format of holding the fall meeting in Ann Arbor and the spring one at a different location was adopted—with a series of outside speakers (often current managers) presenting at the spring meeting.

There are not many references to the IAC in the Regental record, but there are some. For example, in the November and December 1990 minutes there are references to a meeting with the IAC and to the specific advice given. In October 2000, a year after the formation of the stand-alone Chief Investment Office, there is a reference to the IAC being "supportive" of the proposed model portfolio. In October 2001, there is a reference to the Board of Regents consulting with the Investment Advisory Committee semiannually.

The current Investment Advisory Committee Charter is set forth as Appendix Exhibit A2, p. 81, and the current list of IAC members as Appendix Exhibit A3, p. 82.

CHAPTER EIGHT

Working Capital Pools and Other Investments

I n addition to its endowment investments, the University has always held funds that do not constitute "true endowments"—that is, funds whose "principal" is not required to be preserved, but can be spent if required—as well as working capital, or operating, funds central to the University's liquidity plan. It is worth keeping in mind that the term "working capital" is sometimes used as a catch-all to include funds that are not actually being reserved for day-to-day operations as working capital in the strict sense but that also do not fit within the parameters for investment in the endowment's Long Term Portfolio (LTP). For reference, the chart on the next page traces the size of the University's working capital pools from 1930 through 2016, in 2016 dollars according to a CPI index adjustment. Interestingly, for a period (say 1977 through 1993), the working capital pools were actually *larger* than the endowment pools.

Historically, all these funds were called the "University Investment Pool," or UIP,[1] and were, as might be expected, invested in cash or liquid fixed-income securities. For example, in May 1988, the "University Investment Pool Investment Guidelines" were updated from guidelines that restricted the purchase of bank obligations to

---

1 The UIP, now called the Short Term Pool (see below), comprises cash from the schools and colleges expendable accounts; maintenance and construction reserves for dormitories, student residences and other buildings and equipment; and other funds, the principal of which is earmarked to be expended in the reasonably near future.

Real Value of Working Capital Pools 1930–2016

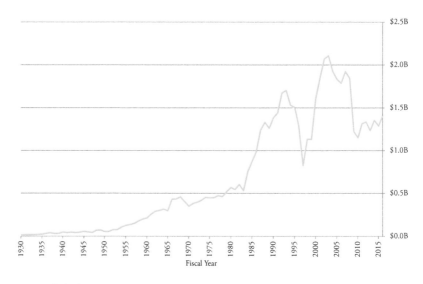

1930-1985: Book value
1986-2016: Market value

banks that are among "the twenty-five largest banks in the country based on deposits" to obligations of banks, holding companies, or thrift institutions that met minimum credit ratings. The item noted: "The requirement of selecting a bank based on
its level of liabilities is inappropriate because this ranking does not reflect the institution's financial soundness." The new guidelines would "provide diversification while
maintaining the high quality rating standard of the University Investment Pool."
Regardless of the modification, this item demonstrates that the UIP was historically
very conservatively invested, with a focus on the preservation of principal.

In November 1992, the UIP guidelines were modified to permit international bond investments, more specifically in the Common Fund's "Global Bond
Fund." The Global Bond Fund made investments in high-quality credit obligations denominated in different currencies worldwide. Much of the item focused
on the potential risks and returns of the non-U.S. currency exposures that could
result from this diversification, although, at the time of this item, the Global
Bond Fund was heavily (80%) weighted to the U.S. dollar.

As described above, April 1994 brought what is probably the most significant
change in policy for the UIP. A large amount of capital, more than $900 million,
had accumulated in the UIP where it was invested primarily in high-quality short

to intermediate maturity fixed-income securities, as well as in three funds (one of which was the Global Bond Fund). This was far in excess of what was needed for working capital purposes and represented, due to the highly conservative nature of the investments, a significant opportunity cost. So it was decided to invest a "permanent core" of the UIP into the endowment portfolio with the expectation of achieving a higher return over time driven by the longer-term, equity-based, and alternative, investments in the University Endowment Fund (UEF).

As part of this change of policy, new accounting constructs were put into place. A new endowment portfolio was created, the Long Term Portfolio, or LTP; the UEF would now become just one participant in the LTP. Also, the concept of "Internal Bank" was introduced. The Internal Bank would sit on top of the UIP by holding investments in working capital portfolios (UIP) as well as the "quasi-endowment" investment in the LTP.[2]

Also described above, in March 2001, the Board of Regents approved an item that confirmed the authority of the Executive Vice President and Chief Financial Officer to designate "Funds Functioning as Endowment" (quasi-endowment) and made it clear that such funds should generally be locked up for a minimum of 5 years. Months later, in October 2001, Internal Bank Procedures were approved by the CFO, adding details to the quasi-endowment policy. It is interesting to note that at this point, the quasi-endowment investment target had been reduced to 25% of Internal Bank assets.

A few years before, in November 1998, another important change had taken place. UIP investments, all fixed income that had been *internally* managed up until this point, were now also given to external managers—many years later than had happened for the endowment investments. The University engaged Pacific Investment Management Company (PIMCO) and Payden & Rygel as active fixed-income managers. A passive manager was to be selected as well.

---

2   Under the "Internal Bank" concept, University units deposit their cash into a common pool—the "bank." Because at any given time the demands on the liquidity of the bank are small relative to its overall assets, a "permanent core" of these assets can be invested in less liquid but higher returning assets, such as are held by the LTP, for example. Similar to a real bank, the deposits represent liabilities. The difference between asset value and liabilities is designated as a "stabilization reserve" (like net equity in a bank). With a current target level of 3% of assets, the stabilization reserve serves as a buffer to absorb variations in the value of the assets. The University units are assured their deposits and are paid a variable short-term interest rate on them. Assuming the reserve levels are satisfied, any investment return above the rate paid to the depositors may be paid annually as a special dividend for allocation by the Executive Vice President and Chief Financial Officer, as well as the President.

In July 2004, the liquid (non-quasi-endowment) investments of the Internal Bank/UIP were reorganized and unitized into two new portfolios: the Daily Portfolio and the Monthly Portfolio. The Daily Portfolio would permit daily liquidity, and the Monthly Portfolio would permit monthly liquidity. The new structure had several advantages: (i) it allowed the University's self-insurance and gift programs to invest into the working capital portfolios (previously these programs had their own portfolios, which was inefficient), (ii) it allowed for cleaner layering by liquidity and risk of the working capital investment program, and (iii) related to the prior point, it allowed the Monthly Portfolio to invest a portion of its assets in "value-add strategies" to supplement its core fixed-income holdings. These value-add strategies would typically be higher returning but often less liquid, although still generally fixed-income oriented.

Thus, in February 2004, the Board of Regents approved the first value-add strategy for the Monthly Portfolio, an investment in Prospect Harbor Credit Partners, a fund managed by an affiliate of Bain Capital. The fund would invest in "non-investment-grade corporate debt . . . primarily in liquid credit instruments including syndicated, floating-rate bank loans; high yield bonds; and credit default swaps."

Going forward from 2004, a portion of the assets of the Monthly Portfolio would be allocated to a diversified portfolio of value-add, income-oriented investments to supplement its core holdings of lower-yielding fixed-income assets.

In October 2008, a more sophisticated, liquidity-based policy for the quasi-endowment investment of the Internal Bank was put into place. According to this policy, which is still in effect today, the "maximum liquidity allocated to the Long Term portfolio will be 60% [of Internal Bank assets], with a trigger for reallocation at 65%."

Starting with 2011, a new internal construct was implemented. Called the "Short-Term Pool" (STP) to contrast with the LTP, the STP simply represented the Internal Bank's investments in the Daily and Monthly Portfolios, thus excluding the Internal Bank's quasi-endowment investment in the LTP. Thus the STP now represents the University's working capital pool. The STP can be viewed as a replacement concept for the UIP, which had become a somewhat confused concept over time due to the various changes we have described. The last reference to the UIP was in the 2009 Report of Investments.

The following table traces how the target allocation for the Internal Bank has changed over time:

CHANGES IN INTERNAL BANK TARGET ALLOCATIONS (%)									
	1998	2000		2005		2009		2015	
Fixed Income (STP)	25	+50	75	−5	70	−30	40	NC	40
Quasi-Endowment (LTP)	75	−50	25	+5	30	+30	60	NC	60

And then the actuals:

CHANGES IN INTERNAL BANK ACTUAL ALLOCATIONS (%)									
	1998	2000		2005		2009		2015	
Fixed Income (STP)	38	+36	74	−8	66	−18	48	−9	39
Quasi-Endowment (LTP)	62	−36	26	+8	34	+18	52	+9	61

And finally the difference between actuals and target:

DIFFERENCE BETWEEN ACTUAL AND TARGET ALLOCATIONS (%)					
	1998	2000	2005	2009	2015
Fixed Income (STP)	+13	−1	−4	+8	−1
Quasi-Endowment (LTP)	−13	+1	+4	−8	+1

Starting in July 2013, a new benchmark was implemented for the Monthly Portfolio. Previously, the benchmark for the Monthly Portfolio had been a value-weighted "roll-up," or consolidation, of the individual benchmarks for each of the funds or separate accounts in the portfolio. There were various issues with this approach. First, the roll-up benchmark by its nature did not provide policy guidance; thus there was no way to perform asset allocation or style attributions. Second, allocating an individual benchmark to some value-add strategies could be arbitrary and problematic. Third, some of the individual benchmarks were not investable. And finally, the roll-up benchmark was required to be changed every time a new manager was added or dropped. Now a true investable policy benchmark was adopted, more analogous to the approach taken with the LTP since the implementation of the Model Portfolio.

The principal endowment portfolio (LTP) and the working capital portfolios (STP) by far make up the bulk of the University's investment assets. Nonetheless, there are some other vehicles of which to be aware. Appendix Exhibit A4, p. 83 sets forth a chart of the University of Michigan's Investment Structure as of June 30, 2016. It shows the LTP, STP, Daily and Monthly Portfolios, the quasi-endowment investment, and the connections between them, all of which we have discussed. In addition, it shows the University's self-insurance vehicles—"Veritas" and the Long-Term Disability (LTD) plan—are invested in the LTP and the Daily and Monthly Portfolios. In addition, there is a set of donor vehicles called "Life Income Funds," which is also invested in the LTP. Finally, there are certain assets that, for various reasons, are invested outside the main portfolios but controlled by the University (see the right side of the chart); these types of assets are broadly designated as "specifically invested." Finally, there are "External Trusts" for which the University is a beneficiary, but these are not controlled by the University and are not consolidated in its financials.

Of course, in addition to investment assets, the University has significant capital assets used in its operations—in particular, real estate (including land), equipment, and library materials. Appendix Exhibit A5, p. 84 sets forth Note 5 of the University's Financial Statements for the fiscal year ending June 30, 2016, listing the value of those assets in broad categories.

CHAPTER NINE

Periodic Reports and Communications to the Board of Regents

The focus of this section is on *current* reports and communications to the Board of Regents, although there is mention of historical practice where appropriate. Note that in February 2005, the old Finance Committee was in effect rechartered as the Finance, Audit & Investment Committee, or FAI Committee, which became the primary contact point for the Chief Investment Office. The FAI Committee is currently composed of three Regents.

REQUESTS FOR ACTION AND ITEMS OF INFORMATION (PERIODIC)

The key categories of communications to the Board of Regents from the University's staff are (i) Requests for Action and (ii) Items of Information. As investing evolved at the University, we have seen that Requests for Action have taken different forms and have addressed a multitude of issues. However, as the endowment model matured, Requests for Action settled into one basic type: the approval of *new* investment managers. This is the practice today.

Items of Information are technically any information that is not requesting action (approval) from the Board of Regents, so they would include the periodic reports described in the following subsections, including the Report of Investments. Apart from these reports, however, the primary Items of Information to the Board of Regents are notifications that the University has invested in new funds with *existing* managers—such investments *not* requiring Board of Regents approval under historical practice.

Especially in recent years, the public nature of both the approval and notification processes has resulted in various instances of undesired attention from the point of view of investment managers who wish to keep aspects of their fundraising, strategy, or the University's participation, confidential. In addition, the ready availability of this information can result in a measure of competitive disadvantage, because other institutional investors have a greater access to information about the University's investments and investing strategy than the University has about them. In certain cases, such as with "Project Ranger" (see p. 53), confidentiality is an absolute precondition to be able to make the investment and, under those circumstances, special delegations from the Board of Regents have been sought.

Note that Michigan's Freedom of Information Act (see pp. 50–51) does not require the current Regental approval and notification processes.[1] It is only because these processes occur subject to the State of Michigan's Open Meetings Act that they take on a public character.

THE REPORT OF INVESTMENTS (ANNUAL)

The Report of Investments (ROI), referenced extensively in this book, has always been the key report about the University's investments. It is delivered to the Board of Regents and to other constituencies.

From 1928 through the 1970s, the ROI was produced primarily once a year as of the closing of the fiscal year in June, although during this period it was sometimes produced twice a year (in June and December). Then in the 1980s through the late 1990s, it was produced twice a year. Then starting in 1999 through today, the Investment Office went back to a single ROI for the fiscal year ending in June. Due to this transition, no ROI was produced during the calendar year of 1998.

---

1   Under the State of Michigan's FOIA and Confidential Research and Investment Information Act, the University is required to make available to the public, annually, a "report of its investments" to include a list of investments. However, this report is only required to be made public once a year; it is not publicized in the same manner as the Regental information and is thus of lesser concern to our current and potential investment managers. The report does serve, however, to meet the public policy of basic disclosure of the University's financial assets.

As might be expected, the content of the ROI has evolved significantly together with the evolution of investing and the changes in structures of the investment portfolios. For example, the 1945 ROI contained the first reference to market values of investments—up until then investments had been reported on a book value basis only. The 1969 ROI contained the first clear references to market value *rates of return*. References to book values were only fully eliminated starting with the June 1992 ROI. Thus, gradually over time, the ROI became less of an accounting report and more of an investment report.

THE MONTHLY INVESTMENT REPORT
FOR THE LONG TERM PORTFOLIO

This typically two-page report is made monthly and summarizes LTP asset allocation, market values, and performance. Once a quarter, it is a couple of pages longer when it incorporates the latest data from alternative asset managers that only report quarterly.

THE MINTS REPORT (ANNUAL)

The item approving the Michigan Investment in New Technology Startups (MINTS) program (direct investing in University technology transfer startups) provides that the "Investment Office shall produce an annual report regarding the MINTS program."

CHAPTER TEN

A Note on the Current Bylaw
Relating to Investing

As part of this history, we have traced key changes to the University's Bylaws as they relate to investing since they were first adopted as resolutions in 1931. Although there have been numerous recastings, renumberings, and reorganizations of the Bylaws, the key changes have been few: (i) in 1952, Finance Committee (of the Board of Regents) approval was no longer required for transactions and (ii) in 1993, the requirement of individual transaction reporting to the Board of Regents was eliminated.

The language of the current Bylaw relating to investing, Bylaw §3.07, by and large, still dates back to 1931; is no longer reflective of how investing is done today; and has a few other technical issues. The focus is still on the execution of individual securities transactions, as opposed to the delegation of investment authority as contemplated under the Uniform Prudent Management of Institutional Funds Act. Nonetheless, the University and its Investment Office have managed to operate under it for many years—primarily by acting in observance of the spirit of the language that two officers (typically the Chief Investment Officer and Chief Financial Officer) jointly execute documentation representing financial commitments of the University, such as the investment documentation for new funds or new separate accounts.

CHAPTER ELEVEN

Conclusion

We do not here recapitulate the summary that was contained in the introduction. But we reiterate that the history and evolution of investing at the University of Michigan is a wonderful case study of how institutional investing generally, and endowment investing in particular, evolved from essentially nothing through today. It is all there, and the different themes have each played their part—from the changes in legal regimes and development of securities markets, through the development of finance and investing theory, as well as the professionalization and specialization, even extreme specialization, of investment managers and strategies, including the development of wholly new asset classes and financial instruments.

As the University closes its fiscal year in June 2016, it holds a Long Term Portfolio that is worth $9.9 billion and is highly diversified geographically as well as in terms of investment strategies, instruments, and number of managers. In fact, as can be seen from the table on the next page, including separate accounts as funds, as of June 30, 2016, the University of Michigan has engaged 284 separate investment management groups[1] and invested in 636 distinct funds or fund-like investments:[2]

---

1 Or equivalent concepts, as appropriate.
2 The concept of "investment vehicle" or investment legal entity is somewhat different than that of "fund" because a single "fund" can include multiple investment vehicles, including alternative investment vehicles set up primarily for tax purposes and co-investment vehicles set up to invest in special projects requiring capital beyond the main fund's capacity.

Number of Managers and Funds by Asset Class
As of June 30, 2016

	Managers	Funds
Daily	1	1
Monthly – Core	3	4
Monthly – Value-Add	15	24
STP Total	**19**	**29**
Fixed Income	4	4
Equity	23	27
Absolute Return	41	78
Private Equity	57	140
Venture Capital	68	164
Real Estate	45	124
Natural Resources	25	69
LTP Total	**263**	**606**
Grand Total	**282**	**635**

Appendix

Exhibit A1 (see p. 52)

UNIFORM PRUDENT MANAGEMENT OF INSTITUTIONAL FUNDS ACT
Act 87 of 2009

AN ACT to establish duties and obligations of nonprofit, charitable institutions in the management and use of funds held for charitable purposes; and to repeal acts and parts of acts.

History: 2009, Act 87, Imd. Eff. Sept. 10, 2009.

The People of the State of Michigan enact:

451.921 Short title.

Sec. 1. This act shall be known and may be cited as the "uniform prudent management of institutional funds act".

History: 2009, Act 87, Imd. Eff. Sept. 10, 2009.

451.922 Definitions.

Sec. 2. As used in this act:

(a) "Charitable purpose" means the relief of poverty, the advancement of education or religion, the promotion of health, the promotion of a governmental purpose, or any other purpose the achievement of which is beneficial to the community.

(b) "Endowment fund" means an institutional fund or part of an institutional fund that, under the terms of a gift instrument, is not wholly expendable by the institution on a current basis. Endowment fund does not include assets that an institution designates as an endowment fund for its own use.

(c) "Gift instrument" means a record or records, including an institutional solicitation, under which property is granted to, transferred to, or held by an institution as an institutional fund.

(d) "Institution" means any of the following:

(*i*) A person, other than an individual, organized and operated exclusively for charitable purposes.

(*ii*) A government or governmental subdivision, agency, or instrumentality, to the extent that it holds funds exclusively for a charitable purpose.

(*iii*) A trust that had both charitable and noncharitable interests, after all noncharitable interests have terminated.

(e) "Institutional fund" means a fund held by an institution exclusively for charitable purposes. Institutional fund does not include any of the following:

(*i*) Program-related assets.

(*ii*) A fund held for an institution by a trustee that is not an institution, unless the fund is held by the trustee as a component trust or fund of a community trust or foundation.

(*iii*) A fund in which a beneficiary that is not an institution has an interest, other than an interest that could arise on violation or failure of the purposes of the fund.

(f) "Person" means an individual, corporation, business trust, estate, trust, partnership, association, joint venture, public corporation, government or governmental subdivision, agency, or instrumentality, or any other legal or commercial entity.

(g) "Program-related asset" means an asset held by an institution primarily to accomplish a charitable purpose of the institution and not primarily for investment.

(h) "Record" means information that is inscribed on a tangible medium or that is stored in an electronic or other medium and is retrievable in perceivable form.

History: 2009, Act 87, Imd. Eff. Sept. 10, 2009.

451.923 Institutional fund; managing and investing; considerations; requirements; pooling 2 or more funds; rules for managing and investing.

Sec. 3. (1) Subject to the intent of a donor expressed in a gift instrument, an institution, in managing and investing an institutional fund, shall consider the charitable purposes of the institution and the purposes of the institutional fund.

(2) In addition to complying with the duty of loyalty imposed by law other than this act, each person responsible for managing and investing an institutional fund shall manage and invest the fund in good faith and with the care an ordinarily prudent person in a like position would exercise under similar circumstances.

(3) In managing and investing an institutional fund, both of the following apply:

(a) An institution may incur only costs that are appropriate and reasonable in relation to the assets, the purposes of the institution, and the skills available to the institution.

(b) An institution shall make a reasonable effort to verify facts relevant to the management and investment of the fund.

(4) An institution may pool 2 or more institutional funds for purposes of management and investment.

(5) Except as otherwise provided by a gift instrument, all of the following rules apply:

(a) In managing and investing an institutional fund, the following factors, if relevant, shall be considered:

(*i*) General economic conditions.

(*ii*) The possible effect of inflation or deflation.

(*iii*) The expected tax consequences, if any, of investment decisions or strategies.

(*iv*) The role that each investment or course of action plays within the overall investment portfolio of the fund.

(*v*) The expected total return from income and the appreciation of investments.

(*vi*) Other resources of the institution.

(*vii*) The needs of the institution and the fund to make distributions and to preserve capital.

(*viii*) An asset's special relationship or special value, if any, to the charitable purposes of the institution.

(b) Management and investment decisions about an individual asset shall not be made in isolation but rather in the context of the institutional fund's portfolio of investments as a whole and as a part of an overall investment strategy having risk and return objectives reasonably suited to the fund and to the institution.

(c) Except as otherwise provided by law other than this act, an institution may invest in any kind of property or type of investment consistent with this section.

(d) An institution shall diversify the investments of an institutional fund unless the institution reasonably determines that, because of special circumstances, the purposes of the fund are better served without diversification.

(e) Within a reasonable time after receiving property, an institution shall make and carry out decisions concerning the retention or disposition of the property or to rebalance a portfolio, in order to bring the institutional fund into compliance with the purposes, terms, and distribution requirements of the institution as necessary to meet other circumstances of the institution and the requirements of this act.

(f) A person that has special skills or expertise, or is selected in reliance upon the person's representation that the person has special skills or expertise, has a duty to use those skills or that expertise in managing and investing institutional funds.

History: 2009, Act 87, Imd. Eff. Sept. 10, 2009.

451.924 Endowment fund assets; appropriation or accumulation; determination; limitation; designation.

Sec. 4. (1) Subject to the intent of a donor expressed in the gift instrument, an institution may appropriate for expenditure or accumulate so much of an endowment fund as the institution determines is prudent for the uses, benefits, purposes, and duration for which the endowment fund is established. Unless stated otherwise in the gift instrument, the assets in an endowment fund are donor-restricted assets until appropriated for expenditure by the institution. In making a determination to appropriate or accumulate, the institution shall act in good faith, with the care that an ordinarily prudent person in a like position would exercise under similar circumstances, and shall consider, if relevant, all of the following factors:

(a) The duration and preservation of the endowment fund.

(b) The purposes of the institution and the endowment fund.

(c) General economic conditions.

(d) The possible effect of inflation or deflation.

(e) The expected total return from income and the appreciation of investments.

(f) Other resources of the institution.

(g) The investment policy of the institution.

(2) To limit the authority to appropriate for expenditure or accumulate under subsection (1), a gift instrument must specifically state the limitation.

(3) Terms in a gift instrument designating a gift as an endowment, or a direction or authorization in the gift instrument to use only "income", "interest", "dividends", "rents, issues, or profits", or "to preserve the principal intact", or words of similar import, do both of the following:

(a) Create an endowment fund of permanent duration unless other language in the gift instrument limits the duration or purpose of the fund.

(b) Do not otherwise limit the authority to appropriate for expenditure or accumulate under subsection (1).

History: 2009, Act 87, Imd. Eff. Sept. 10, 2009.

451.925 Management and investment; delegation to external agent; duty to exercise reasonable care; liability; delegation to committees, officers, or employees.

Sec. 5. (1) Subject to any specific limitation set forth in a gift instrument or in law other than this act, an institution may delegate to an external agent the management and investment of an institutional fund to the extent that an institution could prudently delegate under the circumstances. An institution shall act in good faith, with the care that an ordinarily prudent person in a like position would exercise under similar circumstances, in doing any of the following:

(a) Selecting an agent.

(b) Establishing the scope and terms of the delegation, consistent with the purposes of the institution and the institutional fund.

(c) Periodically reviewing the agent's actions in order to monitor the agent's performance and compliance with the scope and terms of the delegation.

(2) In performing a delegated function, an agent owes a duty to the institution to exercise reasonable care to comply with the scope and terms of the delegation.

(3) An institution that complies with subsection (1) is not liable for the decisions or actions of an agent to which the function was delegated.

(4) By accepting delegation of a management or investment function from an institution that is subject to the laws of this state, an agent submits to the jurisdiction of the courts of this state in all proceedings arising from or related to the delegation or the performance of the delegated function.

(5) An institution may delegate management and investment functions to its committees, officers, or employees as authorized by law of this state other than this act.

History: 2009, Act 87, Imd. Eff. Sept. 10, 2009.

451.926 Release or modification of restriction.

Sec. 6. (1) If the donor consents in a record, an institution may release or modify, in whole or in part, a restriction contained in a gift instrument on the management, investment, or purpose of an institutional fund. A donor may give prior consent to an institution for release or modification of a restriction or charitable purpose in a gift instrument that also includes a restriction or stated charitable purpose subject to this section. A release or modification shall not allow a fund to be used for a purpose other than a charitable purpose of the institution.

(2) A court, on application of an institution, may modify a restriction contained in a gift instrument regarding the management or investment of an institutional fund if the restriction has become impracticable or wasteful, if it impairs the management or investment of the fund, or if, because of circumstances not anticipated by the donor, a modification of a restriction will further the purposes of the fund. The institution shall notify the attorney general of the application, and the attorney general shall be given an opportunity to be heard. To the extent practicable, any modification shall be made in accordance with the donor's probable intention.

(3) If a particular charitable purpose or a restriction contained in a gift instrument on the use of an institutional fund becomes unlawful, impracticable, impossible to achieve, or wasteful, a court, upon application of an institution, may modify the purpose of the fund or the restriction on the use of the fund in a manner consistent with the charitable purposes expressed in the gift instrument. The institution shall notify the attorney general of the application, and the attorney general shall be given an opportunity to be heard.

(4) If an institution determines that a restriction contained in a gift instrument on the management, investment, or purpose of an institutional fund is unlawful, impracticable, impossible to achieve, or wasteful, the institution, 60 days after notification to the attorney general, may release or modify the restriction, in whole or in part, if all of the following apply:

(a) The institutional fund subject to the restriction has a total value of less than $25,000.00.

(b) More than 20 years have elapsed since the fund was established.

(c) The institution uses the property in a manner consistent with the charitable purposes expressed in the gift instrument.

(5) This section does not affect the right of a governing body of an institution to exercise the power to modify restrictions contained in a gift instrument as conferred by the institution's governing instruments or by a gift instrument.

History: 2009, Act 87, Imd. Eff. Sept. 10, 2009.

451.927 Compliance with act; existing facts and circumstances.

Sec. 7. Compliance with this act shall be determined in light of the facts and circumstances existing at the time a decision is made or action is taken and not by hindsight.

History: 2009, Act 87, Imd. Eff. Sept. 10, 2009.

451.928 Applicability of act.

Sec. 8. This act applies to institutional funds existing on or established after the effective date of this act. As applied to institutional funds existing on the effective date of this act, this act governs only decisions made or actions taken on or after that date.

History: 2009, Act 87, Imd. Eff. Sept. 10, 2009.

451.929 Electronic signatures.

Sec. 9. This act modifies, limits, and supersedes the electronic signatures in the global and national commerce act, 15 USC 7001 to 7031, but does not modify, limit, or supersede 15 USC 7001(c) or authorize electronic delivery of any of the notices described in 15 USC 7003(b).

History: 2009, Act 87, Imd. Eff. Sept. 10, 2009.

451.930 Uniformity of law.

Sec. 10. In applying and construing this uniform act, consideration shall be given to the need to promote uniformity of the law with respect to its subject matter among states that enact it.

History: 2009, Act 87, Imd. Eff. Sept. 10, 2009.

451.931 Applicability; scope.

Sec. 11. This act applies only to matters included within the meaning of the terms "institution", "institutional fund", and "person" as defined in this act. This act does not apply to or affect the validity, construction, interpretation, effect, administration, or management of any other trust, estate, or applicable governing instrument.

History: 2009, Act 87, Imd. Eff. Sept. 10, 2009.

Exhibit A2 (see p. 61)

UNIVERSITY OF MICHIGAN INVESTMENT OFFICE
INVESTMENT ADVISORY COMMITTEE CHARTER

Composition

The Investment Advisory Committee (IAC) is composed of six (6) to nine (9) members, appointed at the invitation of the Executive Vice President and Chief Financial Officer. Members shall preferably be alumni of the University of Michigan.

Members shall be highly distinguished in their fields. Although it is expected many will be experienced in investments, the University seeks members of diverse backgrounds and complementary expertise.

Members of the IAC are not compensated for their service. Reasonable travel expenses for attendance at IAC meetings are reimbursed upon request.

Terms

Each member is appointed for a five (5) year term, and is eligible for reappointment at expiration of the term. Terms are staggered.

Meetings

The IAC meets at least twice a year, once in the spring and once in the fall. The fall meeting is often held in Ann Arbor. The other meeting(s) will be held at different locations.

Function

The function of the IAC is advisory. It has no decision-making or approval authority over investments, investment managers, or the operations of the Investment Office. The IAC does not vote on any matters.

Members are expected to utilize their investment, business and other expertise and experience to advise on the strategic direction and implementation of the University's investment program. They are expected to serve as resources, both at and outside of meetings (including individual consultations), to support the building of a successful investment program (such as assisting in providing introductions) and in the proper management of an investment office.

Status

Members of the IAC are not considered by the University to be trustees, officers or otherwise persons responsible for managing and investing an institutional fund, or otherwise owe any fiduciary or other legal duties to the University.

Financial Interests and Relationships

Serving on the IAC does not disqualify investment with managers or vehicles sponsored by or affiliated with members.

However, members must disclose any financial interest or relationship they have with any of the University's investment managers or vehicles, or with any investment managers or vehicles the University is considering.

Exhibit A3 (see p. 61)

MEMBERSHIP LIST
UNIVERSITY OF MICHIGAN
INVESTMENT ADVISORY COMMITTEE

James Cheng
Director
Hedgehog Capital Limited

Domenic J. Ferrante
Managing Partner
The Ferrante Group

Beverly Hamilton
Director, mutual funds, nonprofits
Retired President, ARCO Investment Management

J. Ira Harris
Chairman
J. I. Harris & Associates, LLC

Jay C. Hoag
General Partner
Technology Crossover Ventures

Robert C. Jones, CFA
Chairman and CIO
System Two Advisors

Michael J. Levitt
Chief Executive Officer
Kayne Anderson

Sanford R. Robertson
Francisco Partners

Robert S. Taubman
Chairman, President, CEO
Taubman Centers, Inc.

Advisor on Alternative Investments:

Jonathan M. Harris
President
Alternative Investment Management, LLC

Exhibit A4 (see p. 67)

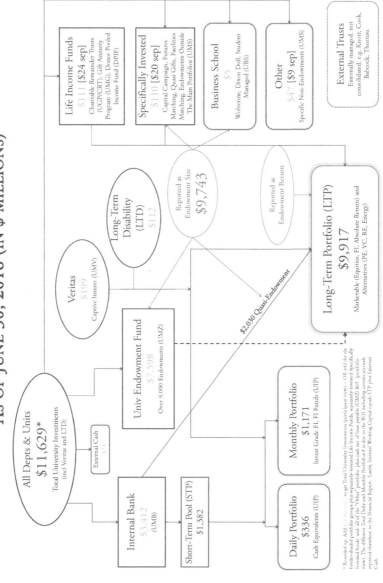

UNIVERSITY OF MICHIGAN INVESTMENT STRUCTURE
AS OF JUNE 30, 2016 (IN $ MILLIONS)

Exhibit A5 (see p. 68)

UNIVERSITY OF MICHIGAN

Notes to Consolidated Financial Statements--Continued

Note 5--Capital Assets

Capital assets activity for the years ended June 30, 2016 and 2015 is summarized as follows:

	2016			
	Beginning Balance	Additions	Retirements	Ending Balance
			(in thousands)	
Land	$ 112,400	$ 1,366	$ 50	$ 113,716
Land improvements	123,003	3,166	1,117	125,052
Infrastructure	248,047	7,132		255,179
Buildings	7,486,312	490,954	20,777	7,956,489
Construction in progress	528,728	(76,581)		452,147
Property held for future use	24,502			24,502
Equipment	1,861,266	142,607	112,006	1,891,867
Library materials	567,461	26,306		593,767
	10,951,719	594,950	133,950	11,412,719
Less accumulated depreciation	5,329,333	501,631	126,821	5,704,143
	$ 5,622,386	$ 93,319	$ 7,129	$ 5,708,576

	2015			
	Beginning Balance	Additions	Retirements	Ending Balance
			(in thousands)	
Land	$ 112,011	$ 389		$ 112,400
Land improvements	116,677	8,564	$ 2,238	123,003
Infrastructure	241,528	6,519		248,047
Buildings	7,283,237	245,727	42,652	7,486,312
Construction in progress	270,963	257,765		528,728
Property held for future use	30,779	(6,277)		24,502
Equipment	1,879,237	122,262	140,233	1,861,266
Library materials	542,672	24,789		567,461
	10,477,104	659,738	185,123	10,951,719
Less accumulated depreciation	5,010,433	493,629	174,729	5,329,333
	$ 5,466,671	$ 166,109	$ 10,394	$ 5,622,386

The decrease in construction in progress of $76,581,000 in 2016 represents the amount of capital expenditures for new projects of $504,099,000 net of assets placed in service of $580,680,000. The increase in construction in progress of $257,765,000 in 2015 represents the amount of capital expenditures for new projects of $585,979,000 net of assets placed in service of $328,214,000.

About the Authors

RAFAEL E. CASTILLA is Director of Investments and Structuring at the University of Michigan Investment Office and has lectured on investment management law at the University of Michigan Law School. He has spent his career in the securities industry and is a CFA charterholder. Rafael is a graduate of Yale Law School (JD 1992) and Harvard College (AB 1989).

WILLIAM P. HODGESON is an Investment Associate at the University of Michigan Investment Office. He has spent his career in the institutional investment management industry and is a CFA charterholder. William is a graduate of the University of Michigan Stephen M. Ross School of Business (MBA 2014) and Saginaw Valley State University (BBA 2008).

Index

Tables, figures, and notes are indicated by *t, f,* and *n,* respectively.

CPSIA information can be obtained
at www.ICGtesting.com
Printed in the USA
LVOW05s1552020817
543320LV00007B/16/P

9 781607 853916